The Little Rock Crisis

The Little Rock Crisis

A Constitutional Interpretation

TONY FREYER

Contributions in Legal Studies, Number 30

GREENWOOD PRESS
WESTPORT, CONNECTICUT · LONDON, ENGLAND

Library of Congress Cataloging in Publication Data

Freyer, Tony Allan.
  The Little Rock crisis.

  (Contributions in legal studies, ISSN 0147-1074 ;
no. 30)
  Includes bibliographical references and index.
  1. Discrimination in education—Law and legislation—
Arkansas—Little Rock.   2. School integration—Arkansas—
Little Rock.   3. Discrimination in education—Law and
legislation—United States.   4. School integration—
United States.   I. Title.   II. Series.
  KFA3992.2.F73   1984   344.767'0798   83-26663
  ISBN 0-313-24416-2 (lib. bdg.)   347.6704798

Library of Congress Catalog Card Number: 83-26663
ISBN: 0-313-24416-2
ISSN: 0147-1074

First published in 1984

Greenwood Press
A division of Congressional Information Service, Inc.
88 Post Road West
Westport, Connecticut 06881

Printed in the United States of America

10 9 8 7 6 5 4 3 2 1

For the Community of Little Rock

But when ye shall hear of wars and commotions, be not terrified: for these things must first come to pass; but the end is not by and by.

St. Luke 21, 9

The facts were not disputed. The order of facts—which came first and which came last, the relations among facts—here he had trouble, but it was not the trouble of facing facts. It was the trouble of understanding them, keeping them straight.

Tim O'Brien, *Going After Cacciato*

Contents _____

Acknowledgments _____

Many have written about Little Rock's 1957–1959 integration troubles. Daisy Bates, Virgil T. Blossom, Brooks Hays, Elizabeth Huckaby, and Orval E. Faubus have provided the perspective of participants. Numan V. Bartley, Elizabeth Jacoway, and Irving J. Spitzberg, Jr., have made incisive scholarly contributions. Although the present study owes much to these works, it is different from them in at least two ways. First, it draws upon sources that to date have not been used in describing and analyzing the Little Rock crisis. These sources include a number of Federal Bureau of Investigation (FBI) reports, manuscript records of the National Association for the Advancement of Colored People (NAACP), and private legal files. Second, this work uses these new sources to approach the integration conflict in terms of the interplay of local politics and judicial process.

I could never have written the study without the assistance of many people and institutions. Dr. Jacoway sparked my interest in the project; I am grateful to her and Dr. Spitzberg for sharing their research with me. I hope this work will contribute in some small way to the massive and path-breaking study of the Little Rock crisis that Dr. Jacoway currently has in progress. Richard C. Butler generously gave of his time on several occasions to discuss the study; I thank him and Leon B. Catlett for permission to use their *Aaron v. Cooper* case files. Professor Georg Iggers helped greatly in developing the NAACP side of the story by answering questions through a lengthy letter and in two interviews. The Honorable Ronald N. Davies also was of immeasurable help in answering questions in long letters and an interview; through him and the FBI I gained access to the FBI material. Wiley Branton provided a useful interview, while also granting permission to examine his record in the Eisenhower Oral History data located at Columbia University and at the Presidential Library in Abilene, Kansas. Mr. Wesley Pruden, Jr., also kindly gave permission to examine and cite his father's interview in this same collection. I thank also the staffs of these two research centers for valuable and courteous assistance. I am grateful to the heirs of Judge Harry J. Lemley's estate for access to his files located in the archives of the University of Arkansas at Little Rock. I owe a special debt to Bobby Roberts, archivist of UALR, for the unswerving and enthusiastic support he has given to all those working in the field of Arkansas history.

I continue to benefit from the incomparable resources of the manuscript divisions of the Library of Congress and Harvard Law School. Again, I am grateful to Erika Chadbourn of the latter institution for research in the Felix Frankfurter Papers. At the Library of Congress I examined the papers of Frankfurter and Harold Burton, and was given access to the restricted correspondence of the NAACP. I wish to thank Jack Greenberg for opening to me the files of the NAACP Legal Defense Fund in New York City. Also invaluable for insight into the NAACP's operations in Arkansas are the Daisy Bates Papers, located in the Archives Division of the State Historical Society of Wisconsin. I want to thank the staff of that superb facility for assistance during the summer of 1981. John Thomas Elliff made possible examination of the Justice Department's involvement in the crisis by allowing me to use and cite his excellent dissertation.

I am also grateful that several participants in the crisis (in addition to those noted above) were willing to discuss with me their role: Orval Faubus, Bex Shaver, William J. Smith, Harold J. Engstrom, Wayne Upton, Ozell Sutton, Henry E. Spitzberg, A. F. House, James Johnson, William Mitchell, and Everett Tucker. Also, Marcus Halbrook of the Arkansas Legislative Council provided some useful leads.

I owe a special debt to Stanley N. Katz, who has supported the project from its earliest stage. Others have been helpful in different ways: Ray Solomon, Michal Belknap, Harri Baker, C. Fred Williams, Deborah Baldwin, Thomas Kaiser, Cal Ledbetter, Ken Emmel, Harry N. Scheiber, Harold Hyman, John Reid, Charles Bolton, Sheldon Hackney, Lee Williams, Dennis J. Hutchinson, Robert Leflar, Maurice G. Baxter, and James Ely.

Participants in the Legal History Program at the University of Wisconsin Law School during the summer of 1981 were also helpful in one session devoted to this project. Willard Hurst, William G. Foster, Jr., and Mark Tushnet read and commented at length on material that has been included in different form in this study. Professor Foster also let me use a very valuable unpublished manuscript concerning integration. Other participants in the program whose comments were of value include Jennifer Nedelsky, Morton J. Horwitz, Stanley Kutler, Stephen Yeazell, Ted Schneyer, Christopher Tomlins, and Janet Lindgren.

Oscar Handlin, Carl J. Guarneri, Charles Grench, Joel R. Williamson, and Karen Ferguson read all or significant portions of the manuscript and gave useful suggestions for its improvement. A portion of the study appeared in the *Arkansas Historical Quarterly*.

I gratefully acknowledge the financial and institutional sources that made this book possible. A grant from Project '87 during the spring of 1980, and several grants from the Arkansas Endowment for the Humanities during 1980–1981 gave me travel funds and provided release time from teaching to carry out most of the basic research. Anthony Dubé of the Arkansas Endowment and John Shelby, head of Research and Sponsored Programs, University of Arkansas at Little Rock, helped greatly in facilitating the use of the AEH funds. I also acknowledge the aid of Glenn Porter in providing office space during the spring of 1980 in the Eleutherian Mills Historical Library in Wilmington, Delaware, as well as the assistance of Nancy Peterson of the Harvard Business School during the winter of the same year.

I wrote the basic draft of the book while in residence at the Charles Warren Center for American Studies, Harvard University, during 1981–1982. I am indebted to Stephan Thernstrom, the center's director, and his assistant, Patricia Denault, for making this a productive year. I also thank Lucinda Draine for typing the innumerable drafts with skill and good cheer. My wife Zu and young son Allan deserve gratitude, too, for leaving the southern land of their birth and coming to the unpredictable environment of Boston so that I could have a year free to write. I want to note, too, the contribution of Tim O'Brien.

I owe a special debt of gratitude to Janice Dawson and her staff in the Law School, University of Alabama, who typed the final drafts of the book. Forrest and Ellen McDonald generously gave of their valuable time to edit the entire manuscript and to clarify its argument. From them I have learned more about the art of writing history than I can say; my one hope is that the quality of this book will reflect the amount of work they have put into it. Mr. Richard Marshall also deserves thanks for bringing the subject to my attention long ago while I was his student.

Finally, I am grateful to Paul Murphy for accepting this book as a contribution to the Legal Studies series, and to Dr. James T. Sabin for expediting the process, which brought light into my life during a particularly dark time.

Despite the aid of these individuals and institutions, I alone, of course, am responsible for what I have written.

Abbreviations Used in the Notes _____

ABCP	Arthur B. Caldwell Papers (University of Arkansas, Fayetteville)
DBP (SHSW, AD)	Daisy Bates Papers (State Historical Society of Wisconsin, Archives Division)
DDEP	Dwight D. Eisenhower Administration Oral History Project (Columbia University)
FFP (HLS)	Justice Felix Frankfurter Papers (Manuscript Division, Harvard Law School)
FFP (LC)	Justice Felix Frankfurter Papers (Library of Congress)
GGIF (UALR, A)	Georg G. Iggers File (University of Arkansas at Little Rock, Archives)
HHBP (LC)	Justice Harold H. Burton Papers (Library of Congress)
JHJLP (UALR, A)	Judge Harry J. Lemley Papers (University of Arkansas at Little Rock, Archives)
LBCF	Leon B. Catlett Files
NAACP LDF	National Association for the Advancement of Colored People Legal Defense Fund (10 Columbus Circle, New York, N.Y.)
RCBF	Richard C. Butler Files
RRLR	*Race Relations Law Reporter*
SSN	*Southern School News*

The Little Rock Crisis

Introduction _____

In 1903 W.E.B. Du Bois declared that the central problem of the twentieth century was the "problem of the color line."[1] The prophetic truth of the Du Bois view was borne out by Derrick A. Bell's conclusion eighty years later that despite progress, especially in the South, America had not yet achieved any "lasting relief from the social pain of racism."[2] I began this book because I wanted to understand better why that pain seemed so resistant to cure. More particularly, I sought a clearer perception of the relationship between change imposed through law and that achieved through the implementation of moral principle. What ecology—the relationship between individuals' values and their sociopolitical environment—retarded or fostered the attainment of racial justice? Approached in this light, the unpredictable consequences of changing the rules governing social relations came to demand primary attention. As with Prohibition, laws aimed at enforcing morality altered society in myriad, unexpected ways; they also generated such opposition that the level of government force needed to quell it created additional conflicts. Thus, even though law could change moral presumptions, it simultaneously created new problems which threatened what the law was expected to achieve in the first place.

THE LEGAL CONTEXT: *BROWN I* AND *BROWN II*

No doubt the most ambitious attempt in twentieth-century America to bring about social change through law was *Brown v. Board of Education of Topeka, Kansas.*[3] The United States Supreme Court's 1954 decision abolished segregation in public schools as an unconstitutional violation of the Fourteenth Amendment. In so doing, the Court overturned the separate-but-equal doctrine that for over half a century had been the law of the land. Handed down in 1896 in *Plessy* v. *Ferguson*, this doctrine held that separate facilities based on race were constitutional as long as they were equal.[4] Only rarely before the end of World War II did the Court limit the reach of *Plessy*. The most notable instance occurred in 1938 in *Missouri ex rel. Gaines* v. *Canada*, where the Court found that the state's refusal to admit a black man to its law school, even though it provided funds for him to acquire a legal education out of state, was not "equal" under the separate-but-equal doctrine.[5]

Between 1945 and 1950 the Court chipped away further at the edifice of segregation. Influencing the justices' cautious course was their concern about, and inability to agree on, the legal ramifications of narrowing the reach of *Plessy*. The scope of private disagreement among members of the Court became public in 1948 in *Sipuel* v. *Oklahoma State Regents*.[6] The facts of the case were similar to those in *Canada*, except that this time it was a black woman, Ada Louise Sipuel, whose application to law school the state had turned down solely on racial grounds. The personal notes of the judges revealed general agreement that the *Sipuel* decision would be similar to the *Canada* ruling; in addition, however, they showed that at least two justices were inclined to question the constitutional validity of the separate-but-equal doctrine itself. The minority justices' position came to the fore when Oklahoma continued to bar the woman's admission on the grounds that the Court's *Canada*-like opinion allowed time to create an equal but separate black law school. The NAACP, as counsel for Sipuel, promptly filed a motion before the Court which sought to compel immediate admission. The Court denied the motion, which led Justices Frank Murphy and Wiley B. Rutledge to dissent. Rutledge was most critical, calling the state's approach to equality a "legal fiction." "Obviously" he said, "no separate law school could be established elsewhere overnight capable of giving petitioner [Sipuel] a legal education equal to that afforded by the state's long established and well-known state university law school."[7]

Internal wrangling over race-related issues generated further dissents in other Supreme Court cases. Reasons for disagreement sometimes involved questions seemingly unconnected with *Plessy*, but nevertheless reflecting concern about the consequences of discrimination. As the federal government's brief noted in one case, "The United States has been embarrassed in the conduct of foreign relations by acts of discrimination taking place in this country."[8] Signaling that at least some members of the Court were willing to challenge the wisdom of maintaining discriminatory racial standards *per se*, the dissents encouraged the NAACP to mount a direct attack on the separate-but-equal doctrine. In 1949 the NAACP filed *McLaurin* v. *Oklahoma State Regents* and *Sweatt* v. *Painter*. The first case involved racial separation in a graduate education program; the second concerned the same problem at the University of Texas Law School.[9] In their brief the NAACP argued first that the states' treatment of blacks violated the equal protection clause of the Fourteenth Amendment. Next, and of greater importance, the NAACP charged point blank that if the Court agreed that the *Plessy* doctrine was at issue, it should be overruled.[10]

The appeal to overturn *Plessy* aroused controversy within the Court. Part of the debate concerned the historical intent of the framers of the Fourteenth Amendment. But the main issue involved the unforeseen implications of reversing a rule that had governed social relations in the South for over fifty years. Some justices wanted the doctrine overturned because any segregation imposed on blacks a "badge of inferiority," a "caste status." Other members of the Court acknowledged the moral question, but were more concerned that integration of elementary and secondary schools might result from the invalidation of the separate-but-equal doctrine. Still others were less preoccupied with the practical consequences than with the reasoning process by which a result was reached. Felix Frankfurter cautioned against a broad opinion, stating flatly that "*Sweatt . . .*

is no *Dred Scott* case." Finally, after considerable discussion and compromise, Chief Justice Fred M. Vinson wrote brief unanimous decisions in both cases holding in favor of the black litigants' rights under the Fourteenth Amendment. He noted, however, that consideration of the constitutional validity of *Plessy* was unnecessary.[11]

The Court's unwillingness to confront *Plessy* squarely aroused uncertainty and encouraged further legal attacks. By expressly ordering state authorities in Texas and Oklahoma to accept blacks in what had been all-white postgraduate programs, the Supreme Court indicated that it would no longer sanction the equalization standard upheld in *Canada*. But the cursory treatment of the separate-but-equal doctrine left open the constitutional status of segregated public elementary and secondary schools. This question divided critics and supporters of racial separation in the North and the South. In 1952 the NAACP filed five cases aimed at settling the controversy by asking the Court to overrule *Plessy* insofar as it applied to public schools.[12]

After initial argument these cases were consolidated under the style of *Brown* v. *Board of Education*. Successive developments delayed a final decision, at first because *Brown I* (as it came to be called) divided the justices on the question of what they should do about *Plessy*. Vinson and others felt constrained by *Sweatt* and *McLaurin*, while the liberal justices saw the decisions as pointing toward a full-scale overruling of segregation. This disagreement led to an order for reargument, which resulted in yet another postponement when Vinson died and was replaced by the former governor of California, Earl Warren. Warren needed time to familiarize himself with the litigation, which meant that the final opinion did not come down until May 17, 1954. During the interim the new chief justice faced the same division among his colleagues that had confronted Vinson. But whereas the Vinson Court had refused to meet the separate-but-equal doctrine head on, under Warren the Court agreed unanimously on the revolutionary constitutional principle of desegregation. What accounted for the turnabout?[13]

In the years after 1954 it became popular wisdom that the Court's decision in *Brown I* was due largely to the unusual persuasive abilities of Chief Justice Warren. Warren, it seemed, became almost solely responsible for making desegregation part of America's constitutional law. The private deliberations of the justices in the *Brown* litigation from 1952 to 1954 revealed, however, that such a view was simplistic. Preoccupation with Warren's role obscured the degree to which the question of enforcing compliance rather than the establishment of desegregation *per se* had to be dealt with before a unanimous opinion was possible in 1954. The Court's private conference notes show that the deadlock that had led to reargument in 1952 arose because of "severe" disagreement over what the remedy should be if *Plessy* were indeed overturned. Vinson particularly was afraid that invalidating the separate-but-equal doctrine would result in the "complete abolition of public schools in some areas."[14] By Warren's arrival in 1953 the standard governing the implementation of desegregation was the central bone of contention among the judges. As Justice Robert H. Jackson observed during the reargument in 1953, "I foresee a generation of litigation if we send [the five cases] back with no standards, and each case has to come here to determine it standard by standard."[15]

Consensus on the wisdom of postponing consideration of the standards-of-compliance issue was central to bringing about the Court's opinion in 1954. The consensus meant that *before* the Court confronted the thorny problem of implementing its opinion, it would hold upon the constitutionality of *Plessy*. Under Vinson, members of the Court had been unwilling to separate the issues of merits and remedy. Warren's considerable talents for fostering compromise were of course instrumental in getting the Court to accept this separation. But it was Warren's personal qualities, in alliance with a legalistic strategy proposed by Justice Frankfurter, that contributed significantly to the *Brown I* result. From *Sipuel* on Frankfurter had cautioned against a broad-gauged attack on separate-but-equal. He had not generally voted with the liberal minority in race cases because, like Jackson and Vinson, he was much concerned about the terms of remedy. However, as it became clear that a majority of the Court was rapidly coalescing in opposition to *Plessy*, Frankfurter searched for a way to support desegregation while at the same time resolving his apprehension. The justice succeeded by agreeing to vote with the majority on the merits, while he suggested a flexible standard that might govern compliance once the Court turned to that question. The standard he proposed, and that accepted by Warren, was "with all deliberate speed."

But Warren established a basis for compromise in another way. He crafted the *Brown I* decision so as to show that *Sweatt, McLaurin,* and other cases pointed toward the overturning of *Plessy.* As the author of the Oklahoma and Texas opinions, Vinson had been unwilling in 1952 to use them to reverse the separate-but-equal doctrine. To the new chief justice, however, these and other precedents demonstrated that racially separate facilities, no matter how equal in form, deprived blacks of certain intangible psychological and sociological qualities inherent in the educational process itself. Such a separation, therefore, constituted a violation of the Fourteenth Amendment. By grounding the Court's decision in precedent, Warren rebutted claims that history mandated segregation. Justice Stanley Reed, probably the last to be won over to what then became a unanimous opinion, explained privately how Warren's approach influenced him. "While there were many considerations that pointed to a dissent," he wrote, "they did not add up to a balance against the Court's opinion. From Canada through . . . Sweatt . . . the factors looking to fair treatment for Negroes are more important than the weight of history."[16]

A year passed before the Court handed down its compliance decree. One reason for delay was the death of Justice Jackson and his replacement by John Marshall Harlan. In addition, members of the Court perceived that immediate action might create trouble in the primary and fall general elections in the southern states. Frankfurter noted this possibility in July 1954 in a letter to Warren; he wrote that the hearings on remedy should be delayed until "the distorting opportunities of a fall election [are] wholly behind us," because "in . . . some of the states segregation is exploited as a political issue."[17] However, once the Court decided *Brown I,* the uncertainties inherent in the decision to postpone determination of the implementation question returned to demand resolution. The justices had in part reached the postponement decision, of course, because they accepted Frankfurter's idea that desegregation should proceed "with all deliberate speed." Now, faced with the need to give some clear meaning to that phrase, its ambiguity fostered dispute within the closed chambers of the Court.

In April 1955 the final hearing on the compliance decree took place. A private memo from Frankfurter on the fourteenth summed up the range of disagreement among his colleagues. The "trick," wrote the justice, was to formulate "criteria not too loose to invite evasion yet with enough 'give' to leave room for variant problems." Several members of the Court wanted to emphasize speed over deliberation and fix a specific date for the completion of desegregation. Frankfurter feared, however, that imposition of such a date would seem "arbitrary," an "imposition of our will" that ignored local diversity, and would "tend to alienate instead of enlist favorable or educable local sentiment."[18] The Court had two days to ponder these sentiments in private before they heard the arguments of the NAACP, the federal government, and the authorities of the southern states. The NAACP wanted the Court to set a date for compliance; the federal government asked for no such date but called for standards demanding a prompt and reasonable start; and the states urged simply that the details of compliance, such as timing, be left to the local federal district courts.

On May 31 the Supreme Court handed down the *Brown II* decision.[19] As one close student of the opinion noted, it "reflected compromise and equivocation in virtually every line."[20] The federal district courts were given responsibility for implementing the "constitutional principles" of *Brown I*. They would do so by dealing with "varied local problems," according to "equitable principles" that were guided by "practical flexibility" in "adjusting and reconciling public and private needs." Even though federal judges were to consider these factors in bringing about the transition to nondiscriminatory schools, compliance could not "be allowed to yield simply because of disagreement" with the constitutional principle of equal justice.[21]

Brown II then set out the standards that should guide the lower federal courts. Local school authorities must make a "good faith," "prompt and reasonable start" toward compliance; what these words meant, however, was left to the district judges to decide. Desegregation should occur at the "earliest practicable date," but delay was acceptable where problems arose involving "administration . . . the physical condition of the school plant, the school transportation system, personnel, revision of school districts and attendance areas into compact units to achieve a system of determining admission to the public schools on a nonracial basis." Finally, the Court distilled the gradual, limited character of its decision in a closing sentence. The four cases combined under the *Brown* style were returned to the lower federal courts to initiate decrees that would open public schools to black students "on a racially nondiscriminatory basis with all deliberate speed."[22]

THE SOCIAL CONTEXT: THE SOUTHERN TRADITION

The imprecise terms of the *Brown II* decree climaxed the Court's decade-long struggle with the race issue. Acceptance of Frankfurter's elusive phrase as the compliance standard revealed just how uncertain the justices were about the means of bringing about desegregation in the South. Members of the Court were aware that the enforcement of *Brown* could stir up political resistance. To meet such a challenge they might have hoped for assistance from the new Eisenhower administration, as suggested by the U.S. Attorney General's brief during the April hearing of 1955. The "responsibility for achieving compliance with the Court's decision . . . does not rest on the judiciary alone," the brief stated. "Every officer and agency of government, federal, state, and local, is likewise charged with the duty of enforcing the Constitution and the rights guaranteed under it."[23] It was clear, however, that the Court had no real understanding of the nature and scope of the South's potential reaction to desegregation.

Southerners' response to *Brown II* did not crystallize immediately.[24] This equivocal reaction, combined with the "deliberate speed" standard, created the possibility that unpredictable forces could disrupt the implementation of desegregation. There were various sources of unpredictability rooted in the South's culture, many of which had little direct bearing on race. Localism, manifested as a general distrust of outsiders and mixed with a touch of paranoia, whether anti-Communist, anti-semitic, or anti-big business, was a dynamic element in southern attitudes. Another dimension of this thinking grew out of an agrarian tradition, which in turn drew upon social conservatism and evangelical Protestantism and embodied paradoxical values of business boosterism and populism. The boosterism reflected a New South committed to government promotion of commerce and industry. Populist assumptions, although maintaining an inherent suspicion of business enterprise and government, nevertheless supported state aid to industrialization as long as it brought improved social services and jobs and was held accountable to the public interest through regulation.

Other emotional, essentially contradictory, elements influenced the South's perception of the federal government. Where federal legislation brought economic benefit, as with the creation of the social security system, the development of the Tennessee Valley Authority, or aid for education and highways, southerners enthusiastically supported national authority. But the use of federal power to enfranchise women or to strengthen organized labor engendered resistance among southerners based on solemn appeals to states' rights. Reflecting this inconsistency, southern politicians could not escape a certain ambivalence: at times they appealed fervently to the Constitution as the touchstone of benign national strength, but on other occasions they attacked the evil of the federal octopus with all the resolution of demagogues. In such an environment political expediency gave words such as *federal*, *states' rights*, and *Constitution* a manifestly symbolic meaning.

Political considerations could also shape popular perceptions of the nature of law itself. At one level, consistent with the regulatory thrust of agrarian populism, "the law" meant little more than the strong arm of the policeman. On another level, when southerners thought of law as the means to achieve economic development, it became a useful tool for bringing about change. And at yet another stratum of meaning, law, identified with states' rights or the Constitution, acquired an absolute, inviolable character. Southern leaders might link any or all of these conceptions to the attainment of a particular political purpose, such as support for, or opposition to, some federal policy. But whatever the purpose, the content of "the law" was malleable until it acquired concrete form in the flux of social circumstances.

To some degree many Americans throughout the nation shared these attitudes. But in the predominantly rural, small-town South of the 1950s they were accentuated; from the time of Thomas Jefferson and Andrew Jackson through the Civil War, Reconstruction, and the populist movement, they had become ingrained in the region's consciousness. Amorphous, often paradoxical and even inconsistent, these values varied in intensity from place to place; inevitably, however, they provided the context for the implementation of social policy, especially one fashioned by federal authorities. After 1955 both the Supreme Court and the nation learned how this culture would influence the enforcement of *Brown* in unexpected ways. Sometimes, as in Baltimore, desegregation proceeded smoothly; elsewhere, as in Mansfield, Texas, state officials defied the Supreme Court and got away with it. The case of Little Rock, Arkansas, was unique: there, authorities at every level accepted (or at least did not oppose) a moderate desegregation plan. Ultimately, however, no one was willing to take full responsibility for implementing this plan, which resulted in a confrontation of near tragic proportions.

NOTES

1. W.E.B. Du Bois, *The Souls of Black Folk* (New York, 1903), 23.

2. Derrick A. Bell, "Civil Rights Lawyers on the Bench," *Yale Law Journal*, 91 (Mar. 1982), 826.

3. 347 U.S. 483 (1954).

4. 163 U.S. 537 (1896).

5. 305 U.S. 337 (1938). Among the most complete treatments of pre–World War II desegregation litigation is Richard Kluger, *Simple Justice: The History of Brown v. Board of Education and Black America's Struggle for Equality* (1976; reprint, New York: Vintage Books, 1977); for example, re *Canada*, see 202–204. Also enlightening, particularly concerning the motivations underlying the Supreme Court's decisional process in early desegregation cases, is Dennis J. Hutchinson, "Unanimity and Desegregation: Decisionmaking in the Supreme Court, 1948–1958," *Georgetown Law Journal*, 68 (Oct. 1979), 4–14. Because Professor Hutchinson's

work is the most complete study of the justices' private papers concerning desegregation cases, I draw upon it almost exclusively below, even though in many instances I have sifted the memos myself. For purposes of convenience, when I quote a justice's words I cite Hutchinson, unless the reference is directly to a court case.

6. 332 U.S. 631 (1948); Hutchinson, "Unanimity," 4–14.

7. *Fisher* v. *Hurst*, 333 U.S. 147, 152 (1948).

8. Hutchinson, "Unanimity," 13.

9. 339 U.S. 637 (1950); 339 U.S. 629 (1950). A third case became part of a trilogy coming to the Court at the same time: *Henderson* v. *U.S.*, 339 U.S. 816 (1950). Because *Henderson* was a federal rather than a state segregation case I have not discussed it here.

10. Hutchinson, "Unanimity," 17–18.

11. Ibid., 19, 22, 24, 26–27.

12. Ibid., 30–51. Four cases were from Virginia, South Carolina, Delaware, and, of course, Kansas. A fifth case, *Bolling* v. *Sharpe*, 347 U.S. 497 (1954), involved segregated schools in the District of Columbia.

13. Hutchinson, "Unanimity," 30–51; I follow Hutchinson in the discussion below. For further insights on Warren's role see G. Edward White, *Earl Warren: A Public Life* (New York, 1982); and for a generally opposing view see Kluger, *Simple Justice*, 543–747.

14. Hutchinson, "Unanimity," 36.

15. Ibid., 39.

16. Ibid., 43.

17. Ibid., 51.

18. Ibid., 52, 53.

19. 349 U.S. 294 (1955).

20. Hutchinson, "Unanimity," 56.

21. 349 U.S. 294 (1955).

22. Ibid.

23. Hutchinson, "Unanimity," 60.

24. The paragraphs below draw on general works in southern history. See, for example, Bertram Wyatt-Brown, *Southern Honor: Ethics and Behavior in the Old South* (New York, 1982); Carl N. Degler, *Place over Time: The Continuity of Southern Distinctiveness* (Baton Rouge, 1977); W. J. Cash, *The Mind of the South* (New York, 1941). See also Numan V. Bartley, *The Rise of Massive Resistance: Race and Politics in the South during the 1950s* (Baton Rouge, 1969); and Elizabeth Jacoway and David R. Colburn, eds., *Southern Businessmen and Desegregation* (Baton Rouge, 1982).

A Moderate City _____ 1

The *Brown* decisions of 1954 and 1955 established the constitutional principle of desegregation in American public education. The decisions were ambiguous, however, as to what would constitute compliance. During the interval between the two Supreme Court decisions, Little Rock school officials voluntarily worked out a plan that embodied a moderate policy on equal opportunity in the city's schools. This moderation rejected both a segregationist and an activist position, embracing instead a principled conservatism that relied on gradualism and tokenism. By May 1955, social and political realities in Arkansas and the Court's action in *Brown II* seemed to sanction this approach to desegregation in Little Rock.

THE BLOSSOM PLAN

On May 18, 1954, the day following the announcement of the Court's first *Brown* decision, Little Rock's school board initiated action with a view toward compliance. The board instructed Virgil T. Blossom, the new superintendent of schools, to develop a plan consistent with the Court's order. Blossom had been appointed superintendent in 1953, after establishing a good record in the administration of the schools of northwestern Arkansas. His record included effective handling of race-related issues under the separate-but-equal doctrine. Once in Little Rock, Superintendent Blossom paid close attention to the progress of the suits that culminated in *Brown* v. *Board of Education*. A former football player and coach with a touch of political ambition, he approached the board's charge with determination and took the lead in formulating the city's desegregation plan. Neither the school board nor the superintendent was enthusiastic about desegregtion, but they voluntarily initiated a plan out of a firm commitment to obey the law. By the end of May, school officials issued a public statement concerning their planning and the commitment behind it.[1]

The planning process took nearly a year. Initially, Blossom thought of beginning desegregation at the grade-school level, but pressure from parent-teacher associations and other factors soon led him to try another approach. By the fall of 1954 his program, known as the Blossom Plan, was being explained in meetings with black and white teachers and administrators. The superintendent verbally outlined the plan as it had evolved to that point. In the eastern part of the city a new all-black junior high school was being built. According to the Blossom Plan, this would instead become an integrated high school (subsequently named Horace Mann High School), and Dunbar, the existing black high school, would become a junior high whose student body would remain black. A second high school (subsequently called Hall High School) was under construction in the western part of Little Rock; it, too, would be integrated on completion, probably in September 1956. The next year the junior high schools would be integrated. The date for integration of the elementary schools was left unclear, but Blossom expected the process to occur more slowly. Finally, the board would outline several school attendance zones throughout the city. Assignment of students to these zones was to be made without regard to race.[2] For several months, Blossom promoted his plan before various white business organizations and black and white parent groups.

In May of 1955, however, a few days before the Court announced *Brown II*, the Little Rock school board published a plan that differed significantly from Blossom's original. This revised Blossom Plan, known as the Little Rock Phase Program, provided for limited integration of only one high school, Little Rock Central, which was prestigious and nationally recognized as

among the country's best. Integration of Central would not occur until September 1957, and would involve only a handful of
black children. A second phase would open the junior high
schools to a few blacks by 1960. No specific date for integration
of the elementary schools was set, but the fall of 1963 was considered a strong possibility. Children would be allowed to
transfer out of districts where their race was in a minority, which
virtually assured that Horace Mann High, when opened, would
be all black. Finally, the Phase Program provided for a selective
screening process that made it certain that only a small number
of black children would attend Central.[3]

There was an ominous flaw in the Phase Program. The loca-
tion of the all-white Hall High School on the west side of town,
where many of the city's prominent and influential professional and business people lived, meant that the community's
leading citizens would have little direct or personal interest in
the integration program. Central, on the other hand, was located in a predominantly working-class neighborhood. Placing
the responsibility for integration on the shoulders of white
working-class families, while the more influential had no such
duty, inevitably generated class tensions.[4]

As if involving the race issue in class tensions were not bad
enough, Blossom compounded the problem in his speeches on
behalf of the Phase Program. The superintendent gave more than
two hundred speeches promoting the plan throughout the city,
but most of these were addressed to business groups whose
members had little direct involvement with the public schools.
At the same time, he made few efforts to tap the influential
moderate support that had given Little Rock a deserved reputation as a progressive city in race relations. When it was suggested that representatives of this moderate bloc of opinion
should be brought into the process of developing the integration plan, Blossom rejected the idea.[5]

Entwined with these problems was another: the public rationale Blossom and the school board gave for their Phase Program. They explicitly denied that Little Rock's move toward
compliance with the Supreme Court's decision was based on
moral principle, stressing instead that their actions were consistent with an absolute minimum of what the law required. Such

a rationale, they believed, was in line with the predominantly moderate character of Little Rock's people and values. Despite "a general, traditional attitude in favor of segregation," Blossom later wrote, "the majority of residents [in Little Rock] were prepared—reluctantly—to accept the United States Supreme Court 1954 school desegregation decision as the law of the land and to initiate a program of gradual integration of Negro students into Central High."[6]

As will become apparent, this justification seemed reasonable in 1954 and 1955. But, like the class problem, the implications of a reliance on legalism deserve close attention. Though the Blossom Plan was developed voluntarily, the publicly announced reasons underlying its formulation focused on compulsion rather than consent. By stressing compulsion, Blossom and the school board appealed to the value of the rule of law, a value which they hoped would transcend disagreement with the principle of integration. They failed to consider, however, that the public's understanding of what constituted "the law" could itself become the object of controversy. Although the value of law could be used to justify an end to segregation, it also could be used to challenge integration. Both support for and criticism of the Blossom Plan, then, depended in part on the public's perception of the legal basis of the Phase Program.[7]

LITTLE ROCK: A PROFILE

By the mid–1950s Little Rock had earned a reputation as a progressive community. Local government in the city was reasonably free from corruption and machine politics. In a state known for its model one-party Democratic rule, Little Rock's established business and professional interests maintained an independent course. The influence of this leadership contributed to the election of Republican local officials, and, on occasion, a Republican mayor. The business community was nationally recognized as among the South's most aggressive in attracting new enterprise and industry. Among New York bond brokers Little Rock held a solid reputation for credit worthiness.[8]

Material conditions indicated a community of considerable

prosperity and comfort. The population was approximately 107,000; of these about 82,000 were white and 25,000 were black. In this population were approximately 28,000 families, of whom 16,000 earned incomes of at least $7,000 and 4,000 earned more than $10,000. The crime rate was low and the city had won national acclaim as one of the nation's cleanest communities. Little Rock's reputation as the "city of roses" rested upon austere but real aesthetic appeal. Through a federally funded urban renewal program, this appeal was maintained as the city absorbed increased population, particularly from rural areas in the state.[9]

Influential civic groups guided the city's prosperity. Those who owned or managed Little Rock's commercial and industrial operations, and the city's professionals, such as lawyers and accountants, along with their spouses, constituted a social and business elite. On the whole these community leaders belonged to long-established families, though newcomers from outside the city periodically became part of the group also. The elite numbered about one thousand people, with a little over thirty persons comprising an inner circle. The city's businessmen and professionals maintained formal and informal contact with each other through the Chamber of Commerce, the Rotary Club, the Community Chest, the Little Rock Country Club, and exclusive fraternities. Little Rock's prominent women were active through such organizations as the Junior League, the Garden Club, and the Aesthetic Club. These familial and organizational connections represented a stable social hierarchy capable of effectively promoting economic development.

World War II was a turning point in Little Rock's economic life. Prior to the war business leaders had been content with limited developmental vision. As the elite's sons and daughters served in the military and learned first hand about the world outside the city and the South in the aftermath of Pearl Harbor, however, a new spirit took hold which by the early 1950s manifested itself in a determination to realize Little Rock's full economic potential. In response to an aggressive promotional campaign, the federal government built a major air force base in the greater Little Rock area. At the same time, the city's Chamber of Commerce helped finance construction of an industrial

park on the edge of town designed to draw out-of-state capital
and business. Tax incentives, subsidies, and special sites made
the enterprise all the more attractive to outsiders. In pursuing
these developmental goals commercial leaders learned the de-
sirability of having a sympathetic local government. The traditional governmental structure in Little Rock was based on a
mayor and wards represented by aldermen. The wards dif-
fused authority throughout the municipal area and fragmented
political power. In order to increase the influence of Pulaski
Heights—the home of many business and professional leaders—the civic elite began a campaign to replace the aldermen-
mayor system with a city manager form of government. Thus,
increased postwar economic activity led to greater political activism as well.

After the war, Little Rock had also established one of the
South's best records in race relations. In 1927 there had been a
lynching, and during World War II a pattern of police brutality
with strong racial overtones had existed. But by the early 1950s—
through the cooperation of interracial business, civic, and religious groups—most outward signs of racial tension had been
removed. Black policemen patrolled the downtown areas of the
black community. Efforts to integrate the city's public transportation system were under way and were completed with only
minor incidents in 1956. The Rock Island Railroad abolished its
separate waiting rooms during this period. Several downtown
department stores ended segregation of drinking fountains and
removed "white" and "colored" signs. Blacks served on juries,
though more commonly in federal than in state or local courts.
Throughout the city, black and white families lived adjacent to
one another without difficulty. Among adults interpersonal exchanges rarely went beyond daily pleasantries and courtesies,
but children of both races played together on a regular basis.[10]

There were other signs of interracial stability and cooperation. Shortly after blacks were admitted to the law school of the
University of Arkansas in Fayetteville in 1948, the university's
medical school in Little Rock voluntarily admitted them too.
Blacks also enrolled without difficulty in the city's University of
Arkansas Graduate Center, where they composed about half of
the total student body. The main branch of the Little Rock pub-

lic library also opened its doors and shelves to blacks in the early 1950s.[11] Of course, none of this meant that in Little Rock there was any fundamental alteration of the social and institutional segregation in racial life that characterized the rest of the South and, in many ways, the rest of the United States. But without question the city and segments of its population were making progress in ameliorating established racial patterns and attitudes.

Several civic interests contributed to this progress. A number of interracial groups in Little Rock actively supported integration. In 1954 the Arkansas chapter of the Southern Regional Council was reorganized on an integrated basis as the Arkansas Council on Human Relations. Arkansas was one of the first southern states to make this change. The council's meetings brought local black and white leaders together to discuss and act on problems of mutual concern. Often these meetings were held in downtown hotels on an integrated basis. Exchanges between ministers led to the formation of a noted civic organization, the Interracial Ministerial Alliance, which, like the Council on Human Relations, favored some measure of integration in public schools and in society generally. The Urban League, formed in part under the leadership of Congressman Brooks Hays, and in the mid–1950s headed by Winthrop Rockefeller, was another prominent forum for interracial cooperation. *Ad hoc* white business groups informally worked with their counterparts among black businessmen to bring about, among other things, the election of a black alderman (an effort that was not successful until the 1960s). The *Arkansas Gazette*, one of the South's oldest and most respected newspapers, supported integration through its editorial policy.[12]

There was also a political dimension. Despite some resistance in the early 1940s, blacks in Arkansas held the franchise and by the early 1950s voted freely both in party primaries and in regular elections. In some parts of the state the black vote was supported by the paternalism of leading whites. Garland County, located about forty miles west of Little Rock and widely recognized as dominated by a powerful political machine, had elected a black alderman. In other counties local sheriffs protected the black franchise to "avoid trouble." This sort of paternalism was especially conspicuous in the Mississippi Delta region of the state, where plantation agriculture had predominated and where a majority of Arkansas blacks lived, outnumbering whites in some areas. The planters protected and controlled this significant black voting bloc through their influence over employment and credit and by granting patronage to local black leaders.[13]

These arrangements operated within the framework of a larger political structure. Majorities in the state legislature grew out of shifting regional alignments of counties; these alignments, in turn, depended in large part on the disbursement of patronage, which to a great extent was funneled through the governor's office. In addition, the county (or blocks of counties) provided the institutional forum for the manifestation of interests, and the governor formulated policies through which these interests might be satisfied. Thus, though the changing alignments might enable a surprise candidate to win one biennial election for governor, he was unlikely to be reelected unless he met the needs of county politicians. Typically, a governor worked to satisfy these needs through legislative initiative during his first term and simultaneously began his campaign for reelection in the party primary, which occurred in the summer of his second year in office. A successful governor was one who could not only operate effectively with immediate political interests, but who could also anticipate new challenges and choose the safest course among competing uncertainties.[14]

Former governor Carl E. Bailey captured the essence of this political culture in a news story in 1954. When "the politicians were divided and disorganized," a candidate could get his "share of factions." But when the candidate ran for reelection as a known quantity, he must have learned to work with the established local politicos. "I can see," said Bailey, "that a man can win a political race without being a politician, but if he's going to survive after he's elected, he's got to become a passable politician. Just working hard, keeping the administration clean and economical and efficient is not enough."[15]

Entwined with such realities was another significant dimension: the sheer excitement of running for office. A noted observer of southern politics conveyed something of this when he wrote, "Politics is a highly personalized game. For a vast majority of southerners playing at politics, it has been not necessarily the democratic process in action, so much as a thoroughly delightful sport."[16]

Few Arkansas governors epitomized the political culture of factionalism, personality, and victory more than Orval Eugene Faubus. Faubus was brought into state politics as part of the liberal administration of Sidney McMath around 1950. The McMath administration had supported programs for increased industrialization and improved social services for a state whose civic backwardness, despite tremendous potential, was well known. A surprise candidate in the Democratic primary of 1954, Faubus defeated Governor Francis Cherry in the fall runoff. Once elected, the man from the mountain county of Madison confronted the political realities described by Bailey.[17]

He advocated a vigorous program of development by sponsoring a necessary but politically explosive increase in taxes. One object of the tax increase was a program of greater aid to education, a marked feature of which was the equalization of salaries and benefits for white and black teachers and administrators. In this and other ways Faubus indicated that, like McMath before him, he recognized the needs and the political value of the black constituency—among others—in his attempt to develop a program to improve economic and social conditions in Arkansas. In a fragmented political environment and as an unexpected victor, Faubus demonstrated that he both supported a progressive development program and was aware of what he had to do to achieve it.[18]

Other developments also reinforced the influence of black voters, particularly in Little Rock. By 1954 the state's Democratic leaders, Faubus among them, had begun a process that made Arkansas the first southern state to appoint blacks to the party's committees. This opened up new channels of patronage that strengthened the influence of black political leaders, especially with the governor's office. Unlike those in East Arkansas and other counties, blacks in Little Rock were relatively independent of white paternalistic control. The city's black leaders knew that their people could be a significant voting bloc, as long as the whites were divided among themselves; Faubus knew from experience in the McMath administration that winning their support entailed directing state and federal funds their way. Just as Little Rock's civic leaders incorporated the interests of middle-class blacks through various interracial groups, the governor cultivated all classes in order to reduce the risks of an uncertain political environment.[19]

Black voters in Little Rock could also influence local elections involving education. The city's school district, like all others in Arkansas, was autonomous. Through popular elections, the inhabitants chose the school board, set some matters of policy, and, within limits established by the state, determined the level of school taxes. A salient fact of school district elections was the low level of voter participation. There were four wards in Little Rock. The first was primarily black, the second and third largely low- and middle-income white. The remaining ward housed most of Little Rock's high-income people, particularly professional and business leaders. Due to the characteristically low turnout of whites in the second and third wards, the voters of the first and fourth, though fewer in number, usually determined the result in local school elections.[20]

RACE RELATIONS

Interracial cooperation and political participation helped minimize the influence of both segregationist and integrationist activists. The Capital Citizens' Council (CCC) was the most vocal group in the community to espouse a strict segregationist position. The city's Citizens' Council was formally organized in April 1955; neither it nor the state-wide organization to which it was related had more than a few hundred members. Indeed, before mid–1955 segregationists in Little Rock and throughout Arkansas were fragmented: they had been unable to cooperate among themselves, to win local elections, to secure passage of measures in the legislature, or to gain influence with newly elected Governor Faubus.[21]

Segregationists, whose leadership and ranks were composed largely of middle- and lower-income people, attributed their lack of success to the "power structure." This structure, according to Amis Guthridge, the CCC's sometime president and lawyer, included the *Arkansas Gazette*, the business groups espousing interracial cooperation, and black groups such as the NAACP. To be sure, the segregationists' populism was buttressed by strong racial views. As a "native of Arkansas and a southerner, I like the negro people," Guthridge said. "But they are different, and that doesn't mean that I think I'm better than they are, or I believe everyone is equal, before God and under law, but some are." Furthermore, Guthridge's perception was that "this whole thing is a conspiracy, and this race mixing thing is part of it . . . it's an effort to side track the people . . . ever since Franklin D. Roosevelt was inaugurated . . . the Commmunists actually took over the operation of the government of the United States from the inside. . . . And they have been determining our policies . . . ever since." Suffusing these beliefs was a distrust of bigness and outsiders, and a fundamental conviction that God's law was being subverted by the dark forces of Satan. Ministers from fundamentalist Protestant sects preached these views among many of the same people who were sympathetic to the message of the Citizens' Council.[22]

The strongest proponent of integration in Little Rock was the local branch of the NAACP. Although the NAACP was considered a militant organization by the standards of the time, its position on how to end segregation in the public schools and in American society generally was actually not radical. The organization opposed direct confrontation and did not promote large-scale civil disobedience. To achieve its goals, the NAACP relied largely on cooperation with sympathetic white organizations and on legal recourse.[23]

The Little Rock branch was part of a loosely structured national organization including two distinct units: the NAACP proper and the Legal Defense and Education Fund of the NAACP. Both were corporations chartered in New York, but they served different functions. The NAACP was a membership organization whose revenues consisted of both membership dues and contributions. The revenues were tax exempt but contributions were not because, under the organization's charter, the NAACP's central purpose was to influence legislation that would help black people.

The Legal Defense Fund (usually known as the Fund or the

Inc. Fund, or simply Inc.) was established as a separate entity within the NAACP in the late 1930s exclusively to engage in litigation on behalf of blacks.[24] That made contributions to it tax exempt for the donor and thus greatly increased its sources of revenue. For a decade after the corporate division, the Inc. Fund continued to operate out of the New York headquarters of the NAACP. Its legal staff was still small, but it had expanded from the late 1930s, when Thurgood Marshall worked with little assistance.[25]

By the mid–1950s the two organizations officially became two distinct entities. The staff, now nominally located at 10 Columbus Circle in New York but actually on the road much of the time, performed most of the legal work done by the Inc. Fund. In addition, twenty-five or thirty lawyers, mostly black and in the southern states, were called upon from time to time to file papers or make court appearances in cases the Fund had taken an interest in. Much of the litigation originated with local black lawyers, the Inc. Fund becoming involved either because its help had been sought or because Fund lawyers, sensing that local efforts were on the wrong track, sought to head off what might lead to a harmful precedent.[26]

The Fund, always behind on paying salaries to its staff in the 1950s, gave top priority to paying rent, phone bills, and travel agencies. When the New York staff worked with a local lawyer, the latter was usually expected to collect his costs and fees, if any, from local sources. A few local black attorneys worked more regularly on projects of special interest to the Fund, and they were occasionally paid something for their services from the meagre resources of the headquarters office. By the mid–1950s this group had emerged as what might be called semi-regular local lawyer affiliates of the Inc. Fund. Their chief work was usually confined to cases in their own communities or states.[27]

The Little Rock NAACP often sought advice and assistance from the national organization, but in most matters it was largely independent. It was small, having no more than a few hundred members, most of whom took little active part. Almost every active member was on the executive committee, which in 1955 included, among others, Rev. J. C. Crenchaw, Mr. and Mrs. L.

C. Bates, Ozell Sutton, and three black attorneys, J. R. Booker, Jackie Shropshire, and Thaddeus W. Williams. Also on the executive committee were two white teachers at the predominantly black Philander Smith College, Drs. Georg G. Iggers and Lee Lorch, whose wives served with them in the organization.[28]

The Little Rock NAACP lacked the will and the support to be strongly militant. Members of the executive committee, for their part, seemingly hoped that racial antagonism would simply disappear as educational and economic opportunities became available to blacks. And, though many blacks in the city doubtless sympathized with the NAACP, they neither supported it financially nor identified openly with it, lest they provoke economic or even physical reprisals from white society. More significantly, some professionals and black teachers were ambivalent about the NAACP. Some of the professionals were involved in the city's interracial business and religious groups, and the state had been upgrading teachers' salaries and benefits. These groups thus had a stake in the dual society. This ambivalence carried over into the black middle-class fraternities and social clubs and into such educational institutions as Philander Smith College. The division was reflected in the black community's two newspapers: the *State Press*, edited by the Bateses, favored the NAACP, while the *Southern Mediator* maintained an accommodationist policy.[29]

The Little Rock branch of the NAACP did have contacts with sympathetic whites in the city and elsewhere in the state. Professor Iggers was a member of the Arkansas Council on Human Relations, and the local branch was influential in the Urban League and in the Interracial Ministerial Alliance. The meeting in the Manor of the Friends (Quakers) was sympathetic to the NAACP. Attending the meeting were not only Quakers, but also Unitarians who left the Unitarian fellowship after blacks were refused membership in 1952. Other whites sympathetic to the NAACP were members of the Pulaski Heights Christian Church. These contacts no doubt contributed, along with the branch's own vigorous efforts, to much of the integration achieved in Little Rock by early 1955. The NAACP had been instrumental in getting black police on patrol in the city's downtown, and the removal of the "white" and "colored" drinking fountain signs in downtown stores was due in large part to NAACP initiative.[30]

These and other successes grew out of and were consistent with Little Rock's pattern of interracial cooperation. When the NAACP went beyond the accepted pattern, however, the results were disappointing. The branch supported a lawsuit to integrate a city hospital, for instance, but the request was denied by the federal court.[31]

An episode that took place in 1952 indicated the limits within which white civic leaders expected the NAACP to operate in its efforts to achieve integration. Early that year Dr. and Mrs. Iggers prepared detailed studies for the branch's educational committee that showed gross inequalities in educational facilities in three Arkansas communities.[32] The most important and extensive study dealt with Little Rock. It focused on the two high schools in the city, Little Rock Central (white) and Dunbar (black). The schools were in easy walking distance of one another, but the report demonstrated that they were far apart academically, in curriculum, and in facilities. The study concluded with the suggestion that inequalities be reduced by allowing Dunbar students to use facilities available at Central but not at Dunbar, such as print shops and other vocational equipment, and by admitting them to courses not offered at their school. Members of the NAACP hoped this might be a first step toward gradual integration. The report was published by an interracial *ad hoc* committee, the Little Rock Council on Schools. The council's membership included representatives of the NAACP, the Urban League, and the Arkansas Council on Human Relations.[33]

The Little Rock school board was willing to discuss the Iggers report with the NAACP, one sympathetic member of the board serving as mediator. At the initial meeting early in 1952, Rev. Lewis Deer of the white suburban Pulaski Heights Christian Church was the spokesman for the NAACP. Three members of the school board were generally favorable; the superintendent of schools was hostile. A second meeting was planned on the understanding that the initiative would remain confidential. To the surprise of the other members of the NAACP,

however, their own attorney, Thaddeus Williams, announced
the planned meeting to the press. The school board immediately canceled the meeting and soon thereafter voted down the
proposal.[34]

This episode pointed up the irony of Little Rock's progressive race relations. As long as the NAACP adopted limited goals
and worked for them quietly and through established interracial channels, the city's civic leadership accommodated it. Any
time it breached those boundaries, however, it could expect to
achieve little and to meet much resistance, from the black community as well as the white. In sum, the very factors that produced stable and steadily improving race relations also assured
that the overthrow of the dual society would take place slowly
if it took place at all.

RACIAL ATTITUDES AND THE LAW

Reinforcing Little Rock's pattern of interracial cooperation were
attitudes concerning race, law, and states' rights. These attitudes produced divergent perceptions of the Supreme Court's
Brown I decision, but they also underscored the community's
fundamentally moderate stance on integration.

It is impossible to delineate all the shades of racial opinion
among Little Rock's whites, but some general observations may
safely be made. Among many working-class whites and among
most activist white segregationists, the common view was that
blacks were biologically inferior. Beyond this presumption,
however, perceptions of the significance of race in regard to social and political arrangements could and did vary considera-
bly. Among the better educated and among professional and
business people, the common view was that it was the blacks'
inferior culture, not genetics, that accounted for their relative
lack of achievement and wealth. From this presumption it log-
ically followed that their "inferiority" would vanish if they were
integrated into white society; but among those with this point
of view, too, there was considerable diversity of opinion on what
social and political changes should be adopted.[35]

The balance of white opinion between those who assumed
biological inferiority and those who favored varying measures

of interracial association was of course uncertain. But the level
and range of interracial organizations and cooperation in Little
Rock by the mid–1950s suggest that, at least among those civic
leaders who were most influential in formulating policies af-
fecting the city's development, the trend of opinion was away
from a stringently segregationist position. At the same time, few
were ready to accept extensive integration throughout the society.[36]

A value contributing to moderation in white views toward race
was community loyalty. Little Rock civic leaders had worked
fervently to develop the city's economy by attracting new industry. This endeavor was not grounded in narrow profiteer-
ing alone; it also reflected pride in building up a community
that had given these leaders a good life and that might, through
more development, give their children a better one. By the mid–
1950s it had become apparent that a good reputation in race relations was helpful in attracting new business. This incentive
no doubt became entwined with sincere and deeply held racial
convictions, as such prominent civic leaders as Winthrop Rockefeller supported institutions of interracial cooperation.[37]

The attitudes of blacks toward Little Rock's race relations, like
those of whites, were varied and difficult to measure. Many
doubtless accepted their status without question; perhaps to do
so is in a person's nature as a social creature. Many doubtless
resented their segregated position, but their number is not as-
certainable, for the dual society required that dissenters play dual
roles, one for white consumption and the other kept bitterly to
themselves. Probably most had mixed feelings, being reluctant
to take on the responsibilities and discomforting wrenches of
integration and yet not accepting the inferior status implied by
legally sanctioned segregation. Certainly middle-class blacks
valued some things more highly than integration. The NAACP
championed the obliteration of a segregated society, but the organization did not hesitate to work within the city's interracial
cooperative network in order to achieve this goal. A direct challenge to segregation through litigation was desirable only as a
last resort. Indirectly, at least, cooperation was consistent with
the moderate character of racial attitudes in the city in general,
and may have indicated a similar opinion concerning race re-

lations held by many of the commmunity's black population.[38]

Related to these racial attitudes were two opposing social theories of law. The first held that "folkways," the patterns of a people's customary behavior and values, were unalterable by law. The idea grew out of Social Darwinism, prevalent at the turn of the century and popularized by Graham Sumner in his book *Folkways*. In the 1950s southerners, among others, restated the folkways theory as "you can't legislate morality." This principle blended with ideas about judicial authority and states' rights to form a comprehensive legal theory challenging the *Brown* decision. *Brown*, in terms of the logic of folkways, was wrong—first, because by reversing the separate-but-equal doctrine, which was consistent with southern tradition, it ordered social change through coercion. Such change, the argument ran, should only occur, if at all, through the normal processes of social experience. Second, the decision was wrong because it embodied ideas about law that had been espoused by Communists and Jews in the North and in foreign countries. Not only were these ideas subversive and alien, but they were used by "outsiders" to stir up blacks who had been content with their lot. Emphasis was also placed on the assumed inferiority of blacks, as shown by their supposed ignorance, general apathy, higher incidence of crime, and family difficulties.[39]

Finally, *Brown* was an unconstitutional usurpation of states' rights by the Supreme Court. *Brown* was unconstitutional because, under the United States Constitution, responsibility for public education was left solely to the states. Thus, in decreeing an end to the separate-but-equal doctrine, the Court was "making law" rather than merely interpreting it. The Court's actions were also unconstitutional because only the United States Congress could pass a law that applied to the entire nation. A Supreme Court decision—like the opinion of any court—applied only to the particular litigants bringing the case; it could become generally applicable to the society at large only when Congress gave it force through legislative enactment.[40]

Karr Shannon, editorial writer for one of Little Rock's two newspapers, the *Arkansas Democrat*, summarized the sociological and legalistic dimensions of the anti-*Brown* theory. The Court, Shannon wrote, "is the nation's judiciary department, endowed with the power to INTERPRET the laws. But in the matter of integration, it went beyond the boundaries of its domain, invaded the authority of Congress—and ENACTED a law." Though Arkansas and other southern states had embraced limited integration, the resentment against the Court grew out of "forced integration . . . based on sociology and psychology, and not on precedent or constitutional edict." To the South this meant the "destruction of states' rights . . . and the federal government, not the elective board, running the local school with mailed fist." At stake were "the rights of the sovereign states, the survival of our republican form of government . . . not the principle of integrated schools." The real issue was "whether these United States are to come under a totalitarian regime with appointive federal judges, not elective officials running the government down to and including the most remote school district."[41]

Those favoring integration propounded their own social theory of law, one that rested on the assumption that law not only enforced, but in fact helped create, social values and institutions. Like the advocates of the folkways theory, integrationists developed a sociological and psychological argument to support their constitutional position. Separate education could not be equal, the argument held, because true education involved important intangibles, such as the opportunity to mingle with and learn from people of varying backgrounds. The argument was first used in a California suit challenging the segregation of Mexican children in public schools; the Supreme Court later invalidated segregation in professional schools using the same argument. In the *Brown* decision, the Court accepted the theory as applicable to elementary and secondary schools. In so doing, the Court implicitly gave its sanction to the idea that law does not merely ratify existing community behavior, but may shape attitudes and create new patterns of human conduct.[42]

Reflecting this spectrum of attitudes and assumptions in Little Rock were three categories of opinion concerning the duty to obey *Brown*. At one end of the spectrum were ardent segregationists. Fired by the conviction that integration was against God's will, a tool of Communists and outsiders, contrary to the desires of most blacks, and an unconstitutional violation of states' rights, segregationists advocated—if necessary—overt resistance to and evasion of the law as defined by the federal courts and as stated in *Brown* (though such resistance, they stressed ambiguously, must remain within the law). In direct opposition were those favoring integration, who preferred a degree and pace of integration in public schools and other parts of community life that was as progressive as possible. They believed that economic incentives would speed popular acceptance of the constitutional principle declared by the Supreme Court, and that when this occurred both races could live together harmoniously, cooperatively, and beneficially.[43]

A third range of opinion, occupying the middle of the spectrum, may be termed moderate. The moderates favored racially segregated schools if allowed by law, but otherwise accepted the need to obey the law through minimum compliance. Moderates believed *Brown* to be unconstitutional but acknowledged that the United States Supreme Court was the final arbiter of the meaning of the Constitution, and thus held that citizens were bound to follow its decrees until the Court changed its opinion. Moderates agreed that blacks should be treated fairly and cordially as a group and as individuals, but felt that because white and black cultures were different, social and educational separation was best for both. Thus taxpayers should support truly equal facilities for both races. Moderate opinion also recognized that certain individual blacks possessed qualities that warranted special recognition. Whites should encourage and accommodate such individuals as fully as possible. Fair treatment of all blacks in general and special recognition of individual blacks contributed to the greater economic development of the community, which was good for all.[44]

Although precise determination is difficult, it seems likely that the moderate view concerning compliance with *Brown* held sway in Little Rock during the winter and spring of 1955. Strong proponents of integration were visible but few in number. Integrationist activism was limited and consistent with a moderate position. Staunch segregationists were even less effective, as was illustrated by the death of several segregation measures in the Arkansas legislative session of 1955. These measures, submitted by East Arkansas representatives, passed the lower house but were defeated on the floor of the senate through parliamentary maneuvering. The defeat revealed the disunity of the state's segregationists and suggested both the influence and the temperament of certain Little Rock voters. Probably in response to the interests of the politically active wards, Little Rock's Senator Max Howell led the opposition and was primarily responsible for the defeat of the legislation.[45]

A moderate course seemed to receive further support in the legal brief prepared by Arkansas for the Supreme Court's hearings in *Brown II*. Local political considerations influenced preparation of the brief. The state's attorney general was nominally in charge of drawing up the arguments, but the brief's contents and approach were formulated by R. B. McCulloch, an attorney from the East Arkansas community of Forrest City. McCulloch, a graduate of Harvard Law School who was recognized among members of the state's bar as a leading constitutional lawyer, had been hired by several Delta school districts to represent their interests. The political influence of the region's representatives insured that he would be given the central role in putting together the Arkansas case.[46]

McCulloch stressed the need for local flexibility and gradual compliance. "We want . . . plenty of elasticity," he said. "What I *don't* want is for the Supreme Court to fix a definite deadline for the completion of integration in all the schools." This assumption suffused the argument Arkansas presented to the Court. The state acknowledged that limited integration would occur immediately (in fact, two Arkansas communities had brought a few blacks into the public schools following the *Brown* decision in 1954). All school boards across the state would make a "prompt start" toward compliance by formulating long-range plans. In general, however, integration would proceed gradually, most schools remaining segregated for the indefinite future. Local school boards would take maximum advantage of pupil assignment laws.[47]

The *Brown II* decision of May 31, 1955, seemed to sanction McCulloch's gradualist approach. Like the Arkansas brief, the Supreme Court's formulation of standards for the enforcement of *Brown I* accepted the necessity for local variations in plans for compliance, left to local administrators and federal judges the development and supervision of integration plans, and (absorbed in the ambiguity of "with all deliberate speed") left open a date for completion of integration. Newspaper surveys after *Brown II* suggested that educational and political leaders in the city and state found the decision acceptable.[48]

In light of *Brown II*, the revised Blossom Plan or Phase Program seemed entirely reasonable, for its shortcomings were not yet apparent. Moreover, it is noteworthy that between the fall of 1954 and May 31, 1955, the school board had revised its plan along lines remarkably consistent with McCulloch's brief. When the Supreme Court sustained the McCulloch argument, it therefore indirectly sanctioned the Blossom Plan. Defeat of the East Arkansas-sponsored segregationist measures in the Arkansas legislature further suggested the appropriateness of the Phase Program. These developments suggested that the school board's integration program was well suited to conditions in Little Rock. School officials had reason to believe that integration would proceed smoothly.

NOTES

1. Virgil T. Blossom, *It Has Happened Here* (New York, 1959), 2, 6, 7, 8, 11. Numan V. Bartley, "Looking Back at Little Rock," *Arkansas Historical Quarterly*, 25 (Summer 1966). Harold Engstrom interview, Dwight D. Eisenhower Administration Oral History Project (Columbia University, 1971), 41, 45 (hereafter DDEP). William G. Cooper, Jr., interview, DDEP (1971), 3. A. F. House interview, DDEP (1971), 10. 1 *Race Relations Law Reporter* 853 (Dec. 1956) (hereafter cited as *RRLR*).

2. Blossom, *It Has Happened Here*, 15–18. Georg G. Iggers, "An Arkansas Professor: The NAACP and the Grass Roots," in *Little Rock, U.S.A.*, ed. Wilson Record and Jane Cassels Record (San Francisco, 1960), 286–287. Georg G. Iggers to Tony Freyer, Sept. 17, 1980, 2–3 (in possession of the author; a copy is located at the University of Arkansas at Little Rock, Archives).

3. Bartley, "Looking Back," 102–103.

4. Ibid., 103–104. Iggers to Freyer, Sept. 17, 1980. Brooks Hays, *A Southern Moderate Speaks* (Chapel Hill, 1959), 184. Orval Eugene Faubus, *Down from the Hills* (Little Rock, 1980), 200.

5. Bartley, "Looking Back," 104–105.

6. Blossom, *It Has Happened Here*, 2; see also p. 14 for Blossom's

statement that this approach was taken after a sampling of the city's
public opinion. The plan was then shaped to conform to those views.

7. Tony A. Freyer, "Politics and Law in the Little Rock Crisis, 1954–
1957," *Arkansas Historical Quarterly*, 40 (Autumn 1981), 195–219. Irving
J. Spitzberg, Jr., "Racial Politics in Little Rock, 1954–1964" (manuscript, 1978), 20, 27.

8. Bartley, "Looking Back," 101–102. Faubus, *Down from the Hills*,
63, 86. Spitzberg, "Racial Politics," 20, 27. Robert R. Brown, *Bigger Than
Little Rock* (Greenwich, Conn., 1958), 1–8. Garry Fullerton, "A Ten-
nessee Newsman: Economic Aftermath," in Record and Record, *Little
Rock, U.S.A.*, 282–283. Boyce Alexander Drummond, Jr., "Arkansas
Politics: A Study of a One-Party System" (Ph.D. diss., University of
Chicago, 1957).

9. This paragraph and the following two paragraphs draw upon
important material in Elizabeth Jacoway, "Taken by Surprise: Little Rock
Business Leaders and Desegregation," in Elizabeth Jacoway and David
R. Colburn, ed., *Southern Businessmen and Desegregation* (Baton Rouge,
1982), 17–19; and the following works: Spitzberg, "Racial Politics," xiii;
Osro Cobb, "*United States* v. *Governor Orval E. Faubus et Al.*" (manuscript, University of Arkansas at Little Rock, Archives, n.d.), in an un-
paged section entitled "The Calm before the Storm"; Daisy Bates, *The
Long Shadow of Little Rock, A Memoir* (New York, 1962), 1–2; A. Stephen Stephan and Charles A. Hicks, "Integration and Segregation in
Arkansas—One Year Afterward," *Journal of Negro Education*, 24 (1955),
172; Brown, *Bigger Than Little Rock*, 1–8.

10. Cobb, "Calm before the Storm"; Bates, *Long Shadow*, 2, 35–38.
Iggers, "Arkansas Professor," 284–285. Ozell Sutton, interview with
author, Nov. 14, 1980.

11. Iggers, "Arkansas Professor," 284.

12. Ibid., 284–285. Cobb, "Calm before the Storm." Bates, *Long
Shadow*, 2, 35–38. Sutton interview, Nov. 14, 1980. See also Brooks Hays,
Politics Is My Parish, An Autobiography (Baton Rouge, 1981), 141; Bart-
ley, "Looking Back," 104; Spitzberg, "Racial Politics," which dis-
cusses at length the civic interests and their attitudes; Stephan and
Hicks, "Integration and Segregation," 183.

13. Drummond, "Arkansas Politics," 50–51, 75–76, 89, 130, 169–186.
Hays, *Politics Is My Parish*, 99-ll4, 138–144. Spitzberg, "Racial Politics,"
20. V. O. Keys, Jr., *Southern Politics* (New York, 1949), 3. Mark Tushnet, memo to author concerning "the NAACP white primary struggle
in the mid–1940s." See also the Arkansas Democratic Primary file in
NAACP Legal Defense Fund, Inc., 10 Columbus Circle, New York
(hereafter NAACP LDF) for correspondence between black Little Rock

attorney Scipio A. Jones and Thurgood Marshall, and other correspondence concerning the NAACP's fight for the franchise. See also
Leon Catlett, interview with author, July 1, 1980.

14. Drummond, "Arkansas Politics," 50–51, 75–76, 89, 130, 138, 169–
186; Hays, *Politics Is My Parish*, 99–114, 138–144; Faubus, *Down from
The Hills*, 24.

15. *Arkansas Recorder*, Dec. 17, 1954.

16. Thomas D. Clark, "Economic Basis of Southern Politics," *Forum*,
112 (Aug. 1949), 86.

17. Faubus, *Down from the Hills*, 13–70. Jim Lester, *A Man for Arkansas: Sid McMath and the Southern Reform Tradition* (Little Rock, 1976), 44,
48, 49, 83, 90, 91, 134.

18. *Southern School News* (hereafter cited as *SSN*), Feb. 3, 1955, 2; Mar.
3, 1955, 2; Apr. 7, 1955, 3; July 6, 1955, 3. Faubus, *Down from the Hills*,
75–92.

19. Drummond, "Arkansas Politics," 91. Faubus, *Down from the Hills*,
11, 79, 87, 148. Spitzberg, "Racial Politics," 20.

20. Spitzberg, "Racial Politics," 13–14. Drummond, "Arkansas Politics," 60–63. Iggers to Freyer, Sept. 17, 1980.

21. Neil R. McMillen, *The Citizens' Council: Organized Resistance to the
Second Reconstruction, 1955–1964* (Urbana, Ill., 1971), 95. Bates, *Long
Shadow*, 80–81. Amis Guthridge interview, DDEP (1972), 10. *SSN*, Mar.
1955, 2; Apr. 1955, 2; July 1955, 3.

22. Guthridge interview, DDEP (1972), 6, 26–27. McMillen, *Citizens'
Council*, 95. Ernest Q. Campbell and Thomas F. Pettigrew, *Christians
in Racial Crisis: A Study of Little Rock's Ministry* (Washington, D.C., 1959),
especially chap. 3. Spitzberg, "Racial Politics," 37–38.

23. Iggers to Freyer, Sept. 17, 1980. Iggers, "Arkansas Professor,"
283–284. Richard Kluger, *Simple Justice: The History of Brown v. Board of
Education and Black America's Struggle for Equality* (1976; reprint, New
York: Vintage Books, 1977), 95–104.

24. "Brief Comparison of Function and Relationship between NAACP
and the Legal Defense and Education Fund of the NAACP, Late 1950s"
(memo from G. W. Foster, Jr., to Tony Freyer, July 17, 1981). Kluger,
Simple Justice, 221–226.

25. Foster to Freyer, "Brief Comparison."

26. Ibid.

27. Ibid.

28. Iggers to Freyer, Sept. 17, 1980. Daisy Bates to Thurgood Marshall, Apr. 6, 1954, in Schools: General File, NAACP LDF.

29. Iggers to Freyer, Sept. 17, 1980. See, generally, G. W. Foster,
Jr., "Turning Point for Desegregation," in Paul Woodring and John

Scanlon, eds., *American Education Today* (New York, 1963), 121–123. See also Kenneth B. Clark, "A Psychologist on the Temper of the Little Rock Negroes," in Record and Record, *Little Rock, U.S.A.*, 25.

30. Iggers to Freyer, Sept. 17, 1980. Iggers, "Arkansas Professor," 284.

31. Johnson v. Crawfis, 1 *RRLR* 151 (U.S.D.C. E.D. Ark. 1955). For early success in white primary fights see reference to Arkansas Democratic Primary file in NAACP LDF. *SSN*, Nov. 1954; Jan. 1955; Feb. 1955.

32. Iggers, "Arkansas Professor," 284–285. Dr. G. G. Iggers, "Dear Fellow Little Rock Citizens," Jan. 29, 1952; and "A Study on Equality under Segregation in the Little Rock Public School System," both in Georg G. Iggers Papers, B–1, File 34, University of Arkansas at Little Rock, Archives, (hereafter cited as GGIF [UALR, A]).

33. Iggers, "A Study on Equality."

34. Iggers to Freyer, Sept. 17, 1980. See also "School Officials Asked to Study Segregation Breakdown Issue," Feb. 1952, newsclipping located in GGIF (UALR, A).

35. There is, of course, a large literature on American and southern racial attitudes which need not be cited at length here. For the sources of these generalized statements as they pertain to Little Rock see Clark, "Psychologist," 259; Campbell and Pettigrew, *Christians in Racial Crisis*, especially 12–13, 14, 40, 60, 104–108, 172–173; Bates, *Long Shadow*, 29, and generally, 6–31; Blossom, *It Has Happened Here*, 18–19; Spitzberg, "Racial Politics," 88–89.

36. Blossom, *It Has Happened Here*, xiii, 14, supports such a view in part. But Spitzberg, "Racial Politics," as a study of the values and actions of the civic elite, is by far the most perceptive statement of the position presented here.

37. Spitzberg, "Racial Politics," xvi-xvii, 26–27, 61, 159–170. Richard C. Butler, interview with author, Jan. 28, 1980; Sutton interview, Nov. 11, 1980.

38. Iggers to Freyer, Sept. 17, 1980; Iggers, "Arkansas Professor," 284.

39. I am indebted to G. W. Foster, Jr., "Education and Law: Segregation in Public Schools" (manuscript, Madison, Wis., 1962), chap. 6, pp. 2–4, for this point. Professor Foster's work is based on numerous interviews with contemporaries in the South during the late 1950s and early 1960s. I am grateful to him for use made of his work here and elsewhere.

40. Ibid., chap. 2, p. 108, chap. 6, pp. 1–25. See also Guthridge interview, DDEP (1972), 18; Faubus, *Down from the Hills*; James S. Johnson, interview with author, Union Life Building, Little Rock, Sept. 4,

1980; Karr Shannon, *Integration Decision Is Unconstitutional* (Little Rock, 1958), 3, 6.

41. Shannon, *Integration Decision Is Unconstitutional*, 3, 6.

42. Kluger, *Simple Justice*, 170–171, 253–254, 264–266, 704–707. Mark Tushnet, "Organizational Politics and Public Interest Law: Two Examples from the NAACP" (paper, 1981), 5.

43. Henry M. Alexander, *The Little Rock Recall Election* (New York, 1960), 3–4. Spitzberg, "Racial Politics," xvi. Blossom, *It Has Happened Here*, 11, 14–15, 22.

44. Alexander, *Recall Election*, 3–4; Spitzberg, "Racial Politics," xvi; Blossom, *It Has Happened Here*, 11, 14–15, 22.

45. *The Americana Annual* (1956), 48. I am indebted to Marcus Halbrook, director of the Arkansas Legislative Council, who wrote this report for the *Annual*, and who discussed the legislation with me in an interview. For basic factual narrative see *SSN*, Mar. 1955, 2; Apr. 1955, 3.

46. *SSN*, Nov. 1954, 2; May 1955, 2; June 1955, 2.

47. *SSN* Nov. 1954, 2; May 1955, 2; June 1955, 2. The McCulloch quote is in R. B. McCulloch to Harry J. Lemley, Sept. 5, 1958, Judge Harry J. Lemley Papers (UALR, A), A–10, Box 2, File 4. See introduction for note on pupil assignment laws.

48. Stephan and Hicks, "Integration and Segregation," 183; *SSN*, June 1955, 2, 13; *Arkansas Gazette*, June 1, 2, 1955.

Aaron v. *Cooper* _____ 2

The Little Rock school board's hopes for uncontested implementation of its integration program were not to be realized.
During the two years prior to the scheduled opening of Central
High on an integrated basis, opposition steadily developed. This
resistance centered on the flaws inherent in the Blossom Plan
and on states' rights ideas that challenged the school board's
legalistic justification for its plan. Further complications arose
from a court case filed against the school board's program, *Aaron* v. *Cooper.* Consideration of the factors that led to this suit
from mid–1955 to mid–1956 establishes a foundation for fuller
understanding of the states' rights challenge.

THE NAACP DECIDES TO SUE

Until the late fall of 1955 there were few if any signs that a
legal challenge to the Blossom Plan was brewing. In August 1954,
Wiley Branton, chairman of the NAACP's Legal Redress Committee, wrote to school board president William G. Cooper, expressing the hope that the board would not adopt a "wait and
see" attitude toward integration, but emphasizing that the
NAACP had "no intention of a suit."[1] In September, representatives of the NAACP and other interracial groups presented a
petition to Virgil Blossom requesting integration. Again, however, there were assurances that there was "no intention of a
suit."[2] Days after the Supreme Court's announcement of *Brown*

II, Mrs. L. C. Bates, president of the Arkansas Conference of Branches of the NAACP, stated that there would be no litigation in areas where school boards moved forward with integration and included the NAACP in the process.[3] In August of 1955 Bates wrote to Cooper urging that integration begin that September. There was no indication of possible litigation.[4]

But during this period of public acquiescence, sentiment within the local NAACP was sharply divided. One group on the branch's executive committee had criticized the Blossom Plan as vague and too limited and had wanted to initiate litigation immediately after the first *Brown* decision. A clear majority of the committee, however, adhered to a more cautious course and voted to give the school board the opportunity to show its good faith. Sentiment against the majority's position shifted only gradually, as it became apparent from newspaper stories that Blossom's Phase Program had undergone major alteration.[5]

Not until the late fall of 1955 did the committee vote to challenge the integration program in court. This shift occurred after it became clear that the new Horace Mann High School would open in February 1956 as a segregated institution. Of further concern was the likelihood that under the proposed transfer guidelines only a handful of black children would be able to attend Central High School. Most black children living near Central would have to walk past the school to reach Horace Mann, some two miles away. Finally, no date was announced for the integration of the rest of Little Rock's public schools.

To prepare a suit contesting this program, the executive committee sought advice from U. Simpson Tate, a Dallas-based attorney affiliated with the NAACP Legal Defense Fund. Georg G. Iggers discussed with him the advisability of seeking an injunction against opening Horace Mann as a segregated school. Tate counseled against this, urging instead that the children living near Central petition for admission there.[6]

The executive committee had turned to Tate in part because of a disagreement with its own local attorney, Thad W. Williams. Williams believed that, given the relatively moderate temperament of race relations in Arkansas, cases should be directed only against those school districts making no effort whatsoever to end segregation. Williams feared that suits against school boards that were voluntarily integrating might result in a "phoney Blossom Plan" being upheld by the federal court. This would encourage other districts to "concoct similar dodges." The local branch of the NAACP was already involved in a suit against the Pulaski County Special School District, where no attempt had been made to comply with *Brown*. Williams thought that the NAACP ought to put all its efforts behind this litigation rather than begin a new case elsewhere. But if the executive committee were committed to the Little Rock case, he counseled that the focus should be the elementary schools, where no date for integration had been announced.[7]

The accommodationist black newspaper, the *Southern Mediator*, editorialized in January 1956 about "some sort" of disagreement within the NAACP over the question of bringing a suit.[8] In fact, some members of the NAACP, working through a sympathetic white attorney, attempted to avoid litigation by urging the school board to return to the integration plan it had discussed in the fall of 1954. But this effort got nowhere, and the executive committee moved forward with its case. Tate advised against Williams's idea of focusing on the elementary schools, and it was decided instead to challenge the inadequacies of the Phase Program. The local branch of the NAACP notified the New York office about its decision. The national headquarters supplied no direct input regarding the suit, but the Legal Defense Fund agreed to review legal briefs prepared by local counsel provided that the local branch pay for its own attorney and bear all other costs. Frank Smith, New York's field representative, played virtually no role, although the branch informed him of its actions.[9]

By January 1956 the executive committee was ready. Before the NAACP could file a case, it was necessary for black parents to attempt to register their children at one or more of the city's schools and for school officials to refuse to register them. Then parents could apply for legal aid. In addition, however, the NAACP needed to raise $300 to hire an attorney. Williams and J. R. Booker, who usually did the Little Rock branch's legal work, were not enthusiastic about serving. Georg Iggers and Lee Lorch, with the full support of the executive committee, took the lead. Iggers suggested, and the committee accepted, a plan for getting parents involved as plaintiffs. On January 23, when Horace Mann High opened, parents would attempt to register children in their neighborhood schools. To locate interested parents, four teams (including, among others, Iggers, Lorch, J. C. Crenchaw, and Mr. and Mrs. L. C. Bates) visited homes throughout black residential areas. The groups found parents supportive of the idea and willing to become parties to it. The parents agreed to gather with their children on the stipulated date at several collection points and attempt to register them.[10] This positive response indicated a change of attitude among the city's blacks, most of whom had not given the NAACP a great deal of support in the past.

Iggers and his wife wrote to family members and friends in the United States and Canada for contributions to finance the Little Rock litigation and build a legal defense fund for other suits throughout the state. Iggers wrote that "public opinion on the whole is moderate" in the city, and it was "likely that school integration can be accomplished with little social tension." But, the professor emphasized, "School board officials, for political and other reasons, are generally unwilling to move unless directed by court order." Even though the school board had announced its willingness to comply with the *Brown* decision, Iggers said, the NAACP considered the board's plan "so vague as to appear more like circumvention than like compliance." A move to file suit was therefore under way because of the impending opening of Horace Mann, "originally announced to be interracial but now restricted to Negroes. As a result . . . several dozen Negro children will be passing the white high school, which at present has no space problem, on their way two miles farther to the new Negro high school." The purpose of the suit was to get the school board to integrate Central and, eventually, Little Rock's other public schools.[11]

The Little Rock NAACP was soon able to procure the services of Wiley Branton, a lawyer in Pine Bluff, about forty-five miles from Little Rock. His work for the Legal Redress Committee took him throughout Arkansas and Mississippi and he was well known to the Little Rock executive committee. His family had lived in Pine Bluff for several generations, was well established in business there, and was on good terms with the white community. The attorney, however, had encountered prejudice both at home and in the military during World War II. Branton's early involvement with the NAACP and its efforts to educate black voters had led to a court case and conviction. The poor quality of his defense had impelled Branton to commit himself to a legal career. He was among the first blacks to graduate from the University of Arkansas School of Law, which had been integrated in 1948. By the mid–1950s, Branton, as one of the few black attorneys in the state, was involved in several NAACP-sponsored cases. The Little Rock suit seemed in no way exceptional.[12]

By the date Horace Mann High School opened, the NAACP, parents, and children were ready to implement the registration plan. The parents—many more than had been approached by the NAACP—gathered at collection points in their neighborhoods and walked to nearby schools. Only a few of the children were from professional or middle-class backgrounds. Most were from working-class families. Because these parents were vulnerble to recrimination (some were employed as service personnel by the school board), several were dissuaded from participating. After attempting to register their children and being turned away, the parents formally appealed to the local NAACP branch for legal aid. The unexpected numbers of parents seeking to participate indicated growing support in the black community for a more activist role by the NAACP.[13]

On February 8, 1956, through the NAACP as legal representative, thirty-three of the children who were not allowed to register filed suit in the United States District Court for the Eastern District of Arkansas. The plaintiff children ranged in age from six to twenty-one; their names appeared on the suit in alphabetical order, the first being John Aaron. The defendants were listed as the president and secretary of the Little Rock School District, the superintendent of schools, and the district itself. The president of the school board was William G. Cooper, a prominent Little Rock physician and civic leader.[14] Upon the filing of *Aaron* v. *Cooper*, members of Little Rock's black community contributed about a thousand dollars in support of the litigation, another indication of a chanᵍe of mood among the city's blacks.[15]

THE SCHOOL BOARD RESPONDS

Superintendent Blossom took charge of meeting the NAACP's legal challenge. He developed a strategy designed both to contest the litigation and to strengthen public support for the Phase Program. The superintendent retained four attorneys in addition to the board's regular counsel, A. F. House, to prepare a defense argument. Each of the four belonged to the capital city's most prestigious law firms. In choosing them Blossom explicitly sought to achieve a representative cross-section of professional opinion concerning integration. He wanted the group to include supporters of the *Brown* decision, opponents of the opinion, and moderates who disagreed with it but accepted it because it was the law of the land. By getting together such a group, he hoped to demonstrate the practicality of Little Rock's integration plan.[16]

Blossom's meeting with Henry E. Spitzberg and Frank E. Chowning to discuss the suit suggests his motivation. The lawyers expressed differing views regarding *Brown* and integration generally. Spitzberg strongly favored the decision and was hopeful about its implications for changing race relations in the South; Chowning disagreed with the Supreme Court's opinion. Blossom replied that "philosophies don't make any difference. I only want to preserve a fine school system." Both lawyers agreed to work on preparing the school board's defense, as did Richard C. Butler and Leon B. Catlett.[17]

Although they disagreed about integration, the four lawyers had much in common. All were well established in prestigious and influential firms, although they were relatively young, being in their forties. They all knew one another to some degree. All were knowledgeable about and involved in politics—local, state, and even national. Generally, their political experience involved organizing for and advising political leaders, rather than service as elected officials. The lawyers were also active in the state and local bar association, connections that often overlapped political ones. They were firmly committed to the civic improvement and economic development of Little Rock, which doubtless influenced their agreement to cooperate in the defense despite their differing views on *Brown*. Perhaps they perceived a connection between a gradual transition in race relations and the general growth of the city. The Phase Program was crucial to such a gradual transition.[18]

Another basis of common experience concerned the nature of the lawyers' practice. During the 1950s in Little Rock, and in Arkansas generally, the typical law firm was not regularly involved in federal court litigation, nor did it spend much time on appeals, even in state courts. Instead, the practice of most Little Rock attorneys involved trial work before local juries, which required mastery of the subtleties of process and procedure but demanded less experience with large issues of jurisprudential theory or constitutional principle. The members of the defense team shared this background, but they had also had solid experience in federal court, both at the trial and the appellate level.[19]

To prepare the school board's defense, then, Blossom had retained men who were both well connected in the city's political and legal establishment and thoroughly equipped to handle the still quite novel legal issues raised by integration. These considerations seemed to enhance the possibility that Blossom could use *Aaron v. Cooper* to foster public support for his plan. It is noteworthy, however, that Blossom focused his attention only on Little Rock's professional elite, ignoring working-class people, whose children would be integrated first.[20]

The school board's regular counsel, A. F. House, was in charge of the attorney group. Born in 1892 and a member of Little Rock's oldest, most established law firm, House was senior to the other lawyers. He had begun his law practice in 1913. Early in his career he became familiar with federal process by litigating insurance cases. House was also thoroughly familiar with local law, having served for four years as a circuit judge for the city of Little Rock. During the 1940s and early 1950s he represented central Arkansas school districts in cases involving education under the separate-but-equal doctrine, especially on issues of salary equalization between white and black teachers and administrators. From this experience House knew that black education was "being neglected"; he felt that the courts had been too lackadaisical in correcting this state of affairs. The son of a Confederate Army veteran, he was perceived among both whites and blacks as a man without prejudice.[21]

House had become the school board's chief counsel in 1952.

He worked with Blossom in preparing to implement the *Brown* decision even before the school board assigned the job to the superintendent in 1954. House agreed with the basic principle established in *Brown*, in part out of a fundamental respect for the authority of the United States Supreme Court. He also welcomed the ambiguity governing compliance as articulated in the phrase "with all deliberate speed." House favored the phrase not because it opened the way to gradualism, but because it provided flexibility for implementing a profound and fundamental change in southern race relations. He read widely, had a deep understanding of law as both a technical and jurisprudential system, and possessed a remarkable ability to gauge the effectiveness of courtroom strategies before trial and appellate judges.[22]

Under House's direction, the attorney group established a systematic program to prepare the school board's defense. As the suit moved to trial during the winter, spring, and summer of 1956, the group held periodic meetings. They communicated among themselves through formal memoranda. From these emerged a discernable strategy that embodied a perception of the case itself and also rested upon certain assumptions about the role of the NAACP and the purpose of integration, and their impact on Little Rock.[23] Shortly after the suit was filed on February 8, House circulated a memo that encompassed what became a basic assumption behind the defense argument. House wrote that the "basic question" for the federal court would be whether it required "slow and orderly" integration or "prompt action with a disregard of the economic and educational factors involved and the possibility of violence." House believed that the court would be "realistic and will look with favor upon any program which will prevent violence and obtain for both negro and white the best educational opportunities."[24]

Two days later House developed another basic assumption of the defense by calling for depositions from the NAACP's local leadership regarding its role. House "generally commended" the NAACP's efforts in "establishing the constitutional rights of negroes." In the present case, however, the issue was not one of constitutional right but of "a good faith acceptance of the right to integrate and the promulgation of a reasonable plan to accomplish that objective." House was convinced that the idea of initiating a suit came from the national office of the NAACP. Headquarters, he believed, had singled out Little Rock as a test case. "It seems to me," the attorney wrote, "that when [the] NAACP comes into a community like Little Rock and starts dictating what is a reasonable time to accomplish integration, it may be opening itself to criticism."[25]

House noted that no black attorney from the capital city had signed the complaint initiating the suit. He interpreted the *Southern Mediator*'s editorial concerning a disagreement between Bates and the Legal Redress Committee to mean that local black attorneys did not generally approve of the "precipitancy of the NAACP." House assumed that local blacks were in a better position to determine the reasonableness of the Blossom Plan than was "an aggressive national organization." Depositions would probably show "a diversity of opinion as to the timing of the suit . . . [and] that local conditions have been subordinated to the aggressiveness of the national leaders." Demonstrating the existence of such diversity, House concluded, might help convince the federal court that "reasonableness is on our side."[26]

The attorney group worked out other aspects of the case. Following Spitzberg's suggestion, Blossom wrote to school districts across the South whose positions on integration were comparable to Little Rock's. Information gathered from these districts was intended to establish the good faith and comparative reasonableness of the city's Phase Program. Spitzberg also pointed out the need to include in an explanation of the program the extent to which it could be "revised in the interest of public weal and cold realities." To give further substance to these ideas he visited New Orleans to discuss with authorities an integration suit that was taking shape in the federal court there.[27] In addition, House stressed the wisdom of avoiding "any kind of technicality" in preparing for or presenting the defense.[28] These and other factors were considered and worked in, or rejected by the defense attorneys as they put together their case. Primarily, however, their strategy was to show the reasonableness of the Blossom Plan in light of the "aggressiveness" of the national office of the NAACP and the diversity of opinion concerning the suit within the local branch.

PRE-TRIAL MANEUVERS

From March to July of 1956, plaintiffs and defendants corresponded with the judge and clerk of the federal court to set dates for the taking of depositions and for the trial of the case. After some negotiation, May 4 was agreed on for the depositions and August 15 for the trial. During the process, several incidents revealed that each party had some misconceptions about the other. Before the deposition date, House mistakenly sent Wiley Branton a copy of the Blossom Plan as it had evolved by the fall of 1954.[29] That plan, of course, had explicitly set the fall of 1956 as the date for beginning integration in Little Rock. When Branton visited House to discuss the depositions, he said that the plan he had been sent was "a reasonable one and . . . [the] NAACP might go along with it."[30] Upon being told by House of the error, Blossom explained to Branton that the earlier plan had been revised. House then sent memos to his co-counsel explaining the mistake and asking them to check their files and to discard any copy of the 1954 version.[31]

Shortly after the incident, Branton came to realize that House misunderstood the NAACP's motives. The NAACP lawyer wrote to Tate that House was "all wet on the policy of the NAACP as he had the idea that our New York office sent people down into Little Rock which had been selected as part of a planned move for the sole purpose of filing a law suit."[32] Two days later he wrote to Tate, "I thought that they would come up with a more definite plan but they are still standing by the one filed with the answer."[33] This reaffirms that the prime motivation for litigation by the Little Rock branch was to hasten the pace of integration according to a clearly specified schedule.

Another development within the local NAACP also indicates the chief motive behind the suit. Because early in the spring of 1956 an instructor had resigned to accept a higher paying position elsewhere, the school board had discontinued an auto mechanics course at Horace Mann High. This represented a major loss of educational opportunity for Little Rock's black youths. Lorch wrote to Tate about whether to open negotiations with the school board concerning the matter.[34] Branton (not Tate) replied to Lorch's letter. He did not "favor . . . any negotiations . . . and strongly recommend[ed] that the NAACP not carry on any negotiations with the board or school officials concerning . . . [these] matters . . . unless further advised by counsel."[35] The trial date was already set, and Branton did not want the litigation to be complicated by extraneous issues. Practical considerations aside, however, the incident suggests that the fundamental concern of the NAACP was the long-range educational needs of black young people.

More than anything else, the taking of depositions on May 4 revealed the disparity in understanding between the NAACP and the attorney group. Over Branton's opposition, federal judge John E. Miller decided in favor of allowing the interrogation of NAACP leaders.[36] After some deliberation House and his colleagues decided to call only two of them, Rev. J. C. Crenchaw, the president of the Little Rock NAACP, and Mrs. L. C. Bates, the president of the Arkansas conference of the organization. House also requested, and Judge Miller allowed, that all correspondence between the local NAACP and the national office be entered as evidence. The school board's attorney knew that Branton could exempt some correspondence from the record because it involved confidentiality between lawyer and client. The rest of it, however, could not be excluded. House was certain that this would show the diversity of opinion within the local branch and the aggressiveness of the national NAACP, and thus "prove helpful."[37]

Branton did have good reasons for not wanting the NAACP's internal affairs aired in public, though they were not the ones envisioned by House. There was, of course, the "disagreement" reported in the *Southern Mediator*. This had not involved local versus national NAACP opinion, but it did show that some committee members favored a different litigation strategy. Any revelation of a break in solidarity could damage the plaintiffs' case. In addition, the deposition proceedings threatened to bring to light other embarrassing facts, especially regarding Tate. Tate's role in preparing the case reflected the less than enthusiastic support shown by the Legal Defense Fund and the NAACP's New York general office. When members of the local branch had asked for his advice, the Dallas lawyer had rarely responded by showing any awareness of or concern about the situation in Little Rock. When Branton raised questions concerning House's mix-up of the two plans and the depositions, Tate replied only in general terms about the authority of the federal court.[38] Branton may also have been concerned about appearing disrespectful of Tate's senior status in the NAACP legal defense organization.[39] Crenchaw wrote to Branton concerning his appearance at the deposition proceeding: "Since the defendants had five (5) law firms representing them the least we could do would be to have two (2) lawyers present." The branch president stressed that "we regard you as the local attorney in charge in this case. . . . The fact is we want you both [Branton and Tate] present."[40] Branton did not accept categorization as local counsel "in charge" of the case: "Let me make it perfectly clear that I regard Mr. Tate as chief counsel in this matter and it is a question of whether the Little Rock Branch desires to have me come up and assist Mr. Tate, rather than Mr. Tate assisting me."[41] These considerations were enough to justify Branton's attempt to quash the taking of depositions.

Judge Miller having rejected the attempt, the proceedings took place on schedule. The attorney group chose Leon Catlett to question Bates and Crenchaw. Members of the Arkansas Bar recognized Catlett as perhaps the most effective trial lawyer in the state. He was active on the state's Democratic committee, knew first hand how politics worked on the grass-roots level, and was experienced in both federal and state court practice. At the May 4 hearing only Butler was absent (for reasons of illness) from the attorney group.[42] Bates and Crenchaw were represented by Branton; Tate was not present. Blossom, too, was there. Catlett questioned each witness separately, after which came cross-examination. House advised that there be "no criticism whatsoever" of the NAACP. The organization "seems to be sacrosanct in the eyes of [Justices] Douglas, Warren, et al., and any skirmish might be viewed in the appellate court as an indication of a reluctance on the part of the district to integrate at a reasonable pace."[43]

The attorney group had prepared about eighty questions to ask Bates and about forty to ask Crenchaw. Following this strategy, Catlett attempted to elicit answers that suggested the inherent reasonableness of the Phase Program.[44] On the whole, however, the responses were inconclusive. Neither witness could remember when the executive committee had discussed bringing the *Aaron* suit or exactly who had voted in favor of the action. They were also unable to remember whether any minutes had been taken during the discussion. Thus, they had no correspondence or other evidence to turn over to the defense. Crenchaw did admit that he had never seen a copy of the Blossom Plan and that he did not know of its precise terms. He said, furthermore, that he was not interested in seeing any plan unless it provided for integration "now." Bates agreed. She admitted that the school board had been courteous and cooperative in meetings with the NAACP. But this did not obscure the fact that extensive segregation was—and would continue to be for years—the dominant characteristic of Little Rock's school system. Such segregation placed heavy burdens on black children and deprived them of educational opportunity.[45]

Catlett's questioning demonstrated that the motives of the two civil rights leaders were grounded in conviction. Crenchaw asserted that if "you start with all on one level and they all know the same thing . . . nobody is being put to any particular disadvantage, but if you push one group forward and one group back, somebody is hurt there and as a National Association for the Advancement of Colored People, we figure we were [*sic*] the ones being hurt." Bates was more concrete. Many black children were bused across town, "being denied . . . the right to attend the school nearest their home." They were denied this right, she emphasized, solely because of race.[46]

Near the end of Bates's interrogation, Catlett asked the conference president to explain the editorial in the *Southern Mediator* about the disagreement between the executive and legal redress committees. Branton objected, claiming that such questions violated confidentiality between lawyer and client, Branton being a member of the Legal Redress Committee. The school board's lawyer asked whether the disagreement explicitly involved the *Aaron* suit; Bates denied that it did. With each attempt to get at the issue, Branton objected.[47] Finally the questioning ended. Branton asked House if he could use his own cross-examination time to interrogate Blossom, even though such a course was not formally scheduled for the hearing. House and the attorney group refused, offering to set another time and date. To the NAACP attorney this refusal seemed inconsiderate.[48]

The most controversial incident to occur at the hearing did not involve strictly legal considerations. During Catlett's questioning of Bates he occasionally referred to the NAACP's "nigger" leaders. On occasion he also referred to Mrs. Bates by her first name, Daisy. The witness objected. In response Catlett exclaimed that he would not call her anything.[49] Catlett's words were viewed as insults by the leaders of the NAACP, who wrote to Branton and Tate asking if anything could be done about it. Branton replied that he was "quite surprised and embarrassed at the conduct of a fellow lawyer." He noted that the Canons of Legal Ethics urged that a lawyer "should always treat adverse witnesses . . . with fairness and due consideration."[50] The local NAACP issued a public statement protesting Catlett's behavior and criticizing his "boorish, rude, impertinent, and unethical conduct" as "an insult to every Negro. It shows clearly the contempt in which he holds us and the determination with which he would relegate us to second-class citizens."[51]

The day after the hearing, the *Arkansas Gazette* published an account of the exchange between Bates and Catlett that aroused public interest.[52] One businessman from East Arkansas wrote to Catlett, suggesting how some may have been touched by what happened. "I was amused as I read the *Gazette* this morning, and want to congratulate you on your stand in this matter, the only thing that I think was wrong was that you answered her too mild, make it a little stronger next time."[53] Thus, even though it was essentially only a minor part of preparing for the trial, the incident drew public attention to the litigation. In so doing it stimulated an emotional response to what was already a highly emotional subject.

TRIAL AND DECISION

Between the deposition hearing and the trial date of August 15, plaintiffs and defendants prepared and submitted briefs to the federal court. The plaintiffs' argument charged that by maintaining a segregated school system Little Rock's school officials had conspired to deprive black children of their constitutional rights. They asked the court for a decree defining the children's rights and for an injunction against enforcing state laws or constitutional provisions that sanctioned segregation. Supporting these points, the brief emphasized the vagueness of the Blossom Plan and the hardships it created by preventing children from attending schools nearest their homes. The school board's response denied these charges. It stressed that the Phase Program had been voluntarily formulated to comply with the *Brown* decision. The plan was developed prior to the Supreme Court's announcement of *Brown II*; no effort was made to base it on Arkansas constitutional or statutory provisions. Under the program integration would occur slowly and on a limited scale, taking into account local conditions and attitudes. Eventually, however, integration would come to the city's schools in a way consistent with the Supreme Court's ruling.[54]

Presiding at the trial was Judge John E. Miller. The jurisdiction of Miller's court did not normally include Little Rock, but the chief judge of the federal eighth circuit, Archibald K. Gardner, had assigned Miller to the *Aaron* case because a vacancy existed in the Little Rock federal district court. The vacancy had first arisen when Judge Thomas C. Trimble withdrew himself from the case because of conflict of interest, his son being a member of one of the firms defending the school board. In addition, however, Trimble was in poor health, and resigned soon after the suit was filed. The *Aaron v. Cooper* trial being imminent, Miller was assigned to handle the litigation.[55]

Franklin D. Roosevelt had appointed Miller as a federal judge. Before his appointment he had served in numerous local offices and in both houses of the United States Congress. Never having lost a race, he was considered to be among Arkansas's most successful—and colorful—politicians. A close friend of the state's effective New Deal senator, Joseph T. Robinson, the judge ranked high in Arkansas's political and legal establishment.

Miller frankly acknowledged his disagreement with the *Brown* decision, but honestly applied it because it was the law of the land. In June 1955, shortly after the Supreme Court handed down *Brown II*, Miller summed up his approach. He did not think the Court had the right to "impose its sociological beliefs on others," but there was "no attitude to take other than to en-

force the law as it was declared by the high court."[56] That Miller
was faithful to this creed was indicated by an observation of a
member of the NAACP: the "rather consistent trend of Judge
Miller's decisions on integration ha[s] caused many white
Southerners to see the handwriting on the wall . . . a factor
which will keep down violent expression."[57] Also, the judge
possessed a remarkable ability to write opinions that appellate
courts would sustain.[58]

As a part of the pretrial preparation House had written to
Miller that the "only" question in the case was whether the
Blossom Plan was reasonable in light of local conditions.[59] In
their brief and their argument during the trial the attorney group
pushed this contention. At the trial, Blossom and Cooper testified, maintaining the same position. The school board had
voluntarily made a "prompt start." Blossom's various activities
in promoting his plan could be construed as an effort to shape
it to local needs. The phased approach allowed for a gradual
transition, which seemed consistent with Little Rock's moderate pattern of race relations. All this indicated the plan's reasonableness; it seemed realistic and practical given the conditions in the city.[60]

Given the ambiguity of the standard "with all deliberate
speed" and the great discretion left to federal judges in apply-
ing it, the plaintiffs had much to overcome. Nor were these the
only difficulties encountered by the NAACP in presenting its
case. During much of the preparation of the suit Tate had been
less than totally involved and committed, and that behavior
continued until the trial began. The lawyer arrived in Little Rock
the evening before the trial date. Instead of discussing strategy
with Branton and the local NAACP leadership, he immediately
went to bed. When he appeared in court the next day he devoted his argument solely to the constitutional dimensions of
the case. No reference was made to the vague, limited nature
of the Phase Program or the hardships it created for black children.[61] Tate's argument suggested an emphasis that misconstrued the local NAACP's purpose. The NAACP's brief had
raised constitutional questions, but the local leadership had
hoped to bring about a change in the integration plan consis-

tent with the 1954 version rather than scrap it altogether as unconstitutional.[62]

When Miller handed down his decision on August 28, 1956, the consequences of Tate's emphasis became clear. The judge held that the case involved no constitutional question since the school board based its program on the rule established in *Brown*, not Arkansas law. The primary issue, in the language of *Brown*, concerned "the adequacy of any plans . . . to effectuate a transition to a racially nondiscriminatory school system." Miller found that the Phase Program represented a prompt and reasonable start. "The plan which has been adapted after thorough and conscientious consideration . . . is a plan that will lead to an effective and gradual adjustment of the problem, and ultimately bring about a school system not based on color distinctions." The judge said, furthermore, that failure to approve the plan or interference with its "consummation" would be an "abuse" of the court's discretion "so long as the defendants move in good faith, as they have since immediately after the decision of May 17, 1954, to inaugurate and make effective a racially nondiscriminatory school system."[63]

Miller retained jurisdiction of the suit in order to deal with questions that might arise as the school board carried out its program.[64] This became a feature of the *Aaron* decision as a result of House's action. The day after the trial, House wrote the attorney group that the "weak spot" in the plan was its failure to stipulate precise dates for the integration of the junior high and elementary schools. "To deflect . . . attack, it seems to me it would be wise," the lawyer wrote, "to suggest to Judge Miller that he approve the Plan in its present form, but subject to later modification if it is shown to him that there is any evidence of bad faith in advancing into phases 2 and 3." House considered this a "serious question," especially because he believed it likely that the NAACP would appeal if it lost in the district court. "In following this suggested plan we have nothing to lose and much to gain in the way of winning appellate court approval."[65] House wrote to Miller suggesting his idea and linking it to the defendant's willingness to go along with any appeal the NAACP might consider necessary.[66] As he did with the defendant's argument

in general, Judge Miller incorporated House's suggestion into
his opinion. His decision to do so insured that the federal court
would maintain a continuous role in implementing the Blossom Plan. The NAACP did appeal, and lost, but this process
was not completed until the spring of 1957.[67]

Miller's opinion left room for cautious optimism that integration in Little Rock would occur with little or no trouble. The
city's two major newspapers, which often disagreed on integration matters, reflected this hope. The *Arkansas Democrat* proclaimed that the decision was a "momentous victory. . . .
Common sense, social order and local school authority stand
triumphant [upholding] . . . gradual integration." While considering the decision in a somewhat broader context, the *Arkansas Gazette* noted that "extremists" both for and against integration were "fated" to "attack" the plan because it provided
"a minimum of integration" spread out over a period "that may
run as long as 10 years." But despite extremist criticism the paper observed that the "program has the support of a considerable majority of the citizens of Little Rock of both races, who
accept it as a practical solution to a difficult problem." The paper also suggested that the judicially sanctioned plan might "well
set a pattern for the Upper South and point a way out of the
dilemma that now faces many Southern communities. It takes
into account the social problems inherent in any such transition, and the emotional climate in which school officials must
function. But it turns away from the futile course of defiance of
the legal process . . . which is being urged across the Deep
South."[68]

In spite of the *Gazette*'s hopeful assessment, there were trou-
bling implications in the *Aaron* case. The school board's effort
to voluntarily comply with *Brown* through a limited desegregation plan depended on moderate leadership. Interracial harmony was crucial to the influence of this leadership, but, as first
the NAACP and then members of the black community as a
whole supported legal action, the moderates' status eroded. Little
Rock's blacks resorted to litigation out of a determination to improve the educational opportunity of their children; neither the
initiative for nor the direction of the case came from the

NAACP's national offices. But the depth of local black commitment, combined with the whites' erroneous belief that outsiders were behind the suit, further strained the city's race relations. In addition, publicity arising from Catlett's racial slurs during the questioning of Mrs. Bates and Reverend Crenchaw aggravated an already emotional issue.

But the *Aaron* case raised other questions as well. The school board's rationale for its desegregation plan based compliance with *Brown* solely on the determined conviction that the rule of law was a value that transcended the whites' preference for segregation. In a narrow sense, Judge Miller's decision applied the Supreme Court's "deliberate speed" standard to Little Rock. But even though the federal court upheld the desegregation plan, the case also seemed to suggest that other approaches might be possible under the Court's *Brown II* rule; temporary delay of desegregation could even seem legal, given certain local conditions. If the community's citizens came to believe that "the law of the land" could be applied so as to delay desegregation, the credibility of the school board's legal justification would be undermined. And if this belief became linked with heightened class awareness, opposition to the desegregation of Central High was not unlikely. Such opposition crystalized around a theory of states' rights called *interposition*.

NOTES

1. Wiley Branton to William G. Cooper, Aug. 21, 1954, in Daisy Bates Papers, MS. 523, Box 4, State Historical Society of Wisconsin, Archives Division (hereafter cited as DBP [SHSW, AD]).

2. Little Rock Board of Education—Legal Redress Committee N.A.A.C.P.—Arkansas, Sept. 9, 1954, in Leon B. Catlett Files (hereafter cited as LBCF), *Aaron* v. *Cooper*.

3. *SSN*, June 1955, 2.

4. William G. Cooper to Mrs. L. C. Bates, Aug. 3, 1955, LBCF.

5. Georg G. Iggers, "An Arkansas Professor: The NAACP and the Grass Roots," in *Little Rock, U.S.A.*, ed. Wilson Record and Jane Cassels Record (San Francisco, 1960), 286–287. Georg G. Iggers to Tony Freyer, Sept. 17, 1980 (in possession of the author; a copy is located at the University of Arkansas at Little Rock, Archives). See also *Aaron* v.

Cooper, Depositions of . . . Rev. J. C. Crenchaw and Mrs. L. C. Bates, 96–100, LBCF (cited hereafter as *Depositions*).

6. Lee Lorch to U. Simpson Tate, Dec. 7, 1955, GGIF (UALR, A), B–1, File 34; Iggers, "Arkansas Professor," 287–288; Iggers to Freyer, Sept. 17, 1980.

7. Lorch to Tate, Dec. 7, 1955.

8. Ibid.; *Depositions*, 96.

9. Iggers, "Arkansas Professor," 288–289.

10. Ibid., 289; Iggers to Freyer, Sept. 17, 1980.

11. Georg G. Iggers to "Dear Friends," Jan. 10, 1956, GGIF (UALR, A).

12. Iggers, "Arkansas Professor," 290. Wiley Branton, interview with author, Dec. 11, 1979. "A Look at Dean Branton," *Barrister*, 8 (Nov. 1979), 8–9. Wiley A. Branton to Osro Cobb, Sept. 29, 1955; Wiley A. Branton to H. R. Weaver, Sept. 30, 1955; DBP (SHSW, AD) MS. 523.

13. Iggers, "Arkansas Professor," 289; Iggers to Freyer, Sept. 17, 1980.

14. *Aaron* v. *Cooper*, 1 *RRLR* 851 (U.S.D.C. E.D. Ark. 1956).

15. Iggers, "Arkansas Professor," 289; Iggers to Freyer, Sept. 17, 1980.

16. Author's interviews with A. F. House, June 16, 1980; Henry E. Spitzberg, Sept. 15, 1980; Leon B. Catlett, July 1, 1980; Richard C. Butler, Feb. 5, 1980. See especially Irving J. Spitzberg, Jr., "Racial Politics in Little Rock, 1954–1964" (manuscript, 1978), 35–36.

17. Spitzberg, "Racial Politics," 35–36. Hon. Leon B. Catlett belonged to the firm of Catlett & Henderson; Hon. Frank E. Chowning to Moore, Burrow, Chowning & Mitchell; Hon. A. F. House to Rose, Meek, House, Barron & Nash; and Hon. Henry E. Spitzberg to Spitzberg, Mitchell & Hays. Each lawyer received $5,000 for his work at the trial level, plus expenses.

18. Author's interviews with House, June 16, 1980; H. E. Spitzberg, Sept. 15, 1980; Catlett, July 1, 1980; Butler, Feb. 5, 1980.

19. See note 18 above.

20. For a general discussion of the flaws in the Blossom Plan, see chap. 1.

21. A. F. House interview, DDEP, (1973), 1 ,3 , 5, 12. See also A. F. House, interview with author, June 16, 1980.

22. See note 21 above.

23. The following discussion derives from materials located in the case files of Leon B. Catlett and Richard C. Butler which are used with their permission. Generally, I will cite a specific memo or other correspondence, using the form in note 24; references will be to the Catlett file (LBCF) in most instances. Where reference is to the Butler file, the citation will be RCBF.

24. Memo, House to Attorney Group, Feb. 3, 1956, LBCF.

25. Ibid., Feb. 15, 1956.
26. Ibid.
27. Two memos, H. E. Spitzberg to Attorney Group, Feb. 16, 1956, and Mar. 5, 1956, LBCF. See also miscellaneous letters and questionnaires between Blossom and school districts in New Orleans, Louisiana, and Mobile, Alabama in LBCF.
28. House to Attorney Group, Feb. 15, 1956.
29. House to Attorney Group, Apr. 3, 1956, LBCF. See chap. 1 for discussion of the 1954 plan.
30. Branton to Tate, Apr. 3, 1956, DBP (SHSW, AD), MS. 523, Box 6, Folder 1.
31. House to Attorney Group, Apr. 3, 1956.
32. Branton to Tate, Apr. 3, 1956.
33. Ibid., Apr. 5, 1956.
34. Lorch to Tate, May 19, 1956, GGIF (UALR, A), B–1, File 34.
35. Branton to Lorch, May 20, 1956, GGIF (UALR, A), B–1, File 34.
36. Hon. Judge John E. Miller to Attorneys House and Branton, Apr. 2, 1956, DBP (SHSW, AD), MS. 523, Box 6, Folder 1.
37. Ibid. House to Attorney Group, Apr. 3, 1956; Mar. 9, 1956; Mar. 27, 1956, LBCF.
38. Branton to Tate, Apr. 13, 1956; Tate to Branton, Apr. 14, 1956, DBP (SHSW, AD), MS. 523, Box 6, Folder 1. Briefs of *Aaron* in DBP show that these, although drafted by Branton, were sent to Thurgood Marshall and members of his staff at the NAACP Legal Defense Fund in New York.
39. Branton to Tate, Apr. 13, 1956; Tate to Branton, Apr. 14, 1956.
40. Crenchaw to Branton, Apr. 20, 1956, GGIF (UALR, A), B–1, File 34.
41. Ibid.; Branton to Iggers, Apr. 16, 1956.
42. House to Attorney Group, Mar. 27, 1956, LBCF. See also author's interviews with House, June 16, 1980; H. E. Spitzberg, Sept. 15, 1980; Catlett, July 1, 1980; Butler, Feb. 5, 1980; and Butler to House, May 21, 1956, LBCF.
43. House to Attorney Group, Mar. 23, 1956, LBCF. See Also Branton to Bates and Crenchaw, Apr. 16, 1956, LBCF.
44. Lists of these questions are located in LBCF and RCBF.
45. *Depositions.*
46. Ibid., 25, 73.
47. Ibid., 96–100.
48. Ibid., 112–113.
49. Ibid., 89.
50. Branton to Lorch, May 20, 1956. See also Lorch to Tate, May 19, 1956.

51. Statement by Mrs. L. C. Bates, GGIF (UALR, A), B–1, File 34.

52. Ibid.

53. Chas. D. McKenzie to Catlett, Mar. 5, 1956. See also author's interviews with House, June 16, 1980, H. E. Spitzberg, Sept. 15, 1980; Catlett, July 1, 1980; Butler, Feb. 5, 1980.

54. The briefs, and correspondence concerning them, are located in LBCF. See also *Aaron* v. *Cooper*, 1 *RRLR* 851 (U.S.D.C. E.D. Ark. 1956).

55. *Hope (Arkansas) Star*, June 8, 1955, located in Judge Harry J. Lemley Papers, Box 1, A–10, File 1 (cited hereafter as JHJLP [UALR, A]). See also Butler to House, May 21, 1956, LBCF. *SSN*, Mar. 4, 1956.

56. "Judge Miller to Carry Out Court Ruling," JHJLP (UALR, A), Box 1, A–10, File 1.

57. Anonymous memo in files of NAACP LDF, New York n.d.; copy in possession of the author.

58. Author's interviews with House, June 16, 1980; H. E. Spitzberg, Sept. 15, 1980; Catlett, July 1, 1980; Butler, Feb. 5, 1980.

59. House to Miller, May 11, 1956, LBCF.

60. "Transcript of Proceedings," located in *Aaron* v. *Cooper* File #1, NAACP LDF, New York.

61. Iggers, "Arkansas Professor," 290.

62. "Statement by Rev. J. C. Crenchaw," DBP (SHSW, AD), MS. 523, Box 4.

63. *Aaron* v. *Cooper*, 1 *RRLR* 853, 860 (U.S.D.C. E.D. Ark. 1956).

64. Ibid.

65 . House to Attorney Group, Aug. 16, 1956, RCBF.

66. House to Miller (n.d.), RCBF.

67. The appeal will be discussed in chap. 3. See *Aaron* v. *Cooper*, 243, F.2d 361 (U.S.C.A. 8th Cir. 1957).

68. *Arkansas Democrat*, Aug. 29, 1956, 10; *Arkansas Gazette*, Aug. 29, 1956, 4. See also *SSN*, Sept. 1956, 15.

Interposition _____ 3

According to the doctrine of interposition a state could interject its sovereign power between its citizens and the national government. The doctrine lacked binding authority in the constitutional law of the United States, and it was susceptible to diverse interpretations; but for many Americans it seemed to provide a way to delay or circumvent desegregation. From mid–1955 to mid–1956 Arkansas segregationists forced their perception of the idea to the center of public debate, seeking to undermine the authority of the Supreme Court and the *Brown* decisions.

THE HOXIE EPISODE

Interposition emerged as a political issue during a desegregation struggle in Hoxie, Arkansas. Located in the northeastern part of the state near the Missouri state line and 138 miles from Little Rock, the community had a population of 1,284 and was part of Lawrence County. The town bordered on, but was not part of, the East Arkansas Mississippi Delta region, and was within sight of the Ozark Mountains. Although there were some trucking, lumbering, and cattle raising concerns, and a few merchants, the principal economic staple—as in the Delta—was cotton. There were fourteen black families in Hoxie, nine of which had school-age children; black and white children attended separate schools. Because the black school was located

two blocks from the nearest sewer line, the toilets were outside. The only source of heat was a wood-burning stove. There
was no janitor, so the children were responsible for cleaning
the school. There was one teacher. Black youths of high school
age were bused some sixty miles to the area's largest town, Jo-
nesboro. Black parents yearned to improve these conditions, but
they lacked organization, and several were economically vulnerable because they were dependent on whites for work. There
was no NAACP group in the town.[1]

During the summer of 1955 desegregation came to Hoxie. The
black educational program was part of the town's independent
local school district, which served the agricultural hamlets of the
area. The school for white children was newer than the black
children's school and had facilities adequate for about a thousand students. On June 25, the five-person Hoxie school board
voted unanimously to abandon the separate black school system and to integrate its twenty-five children into the white
school. The reasons given for voluntary desegregation were that
it was "right in the sight of God," necessary because of the *Brown*
decisions, and "cheaper."[2] Schools in this part of Arkansas held
a split semester that started in July, ran for several weeks, re-
cessed for several weeks so that children could help with har-
vesting, then reconvened in the fall. The school board began its
voluntary desegregation during the first session, starting July
11. For approximately three weeks Hoxie's school operated with
favorable response from the community's parents and children
and without incident.[3]

But by early August opposition developed. Herbert Brewer,
a local trucker and farmer, organized a group called the "Citizens Committee Representing Segregation in the Hoxie
Schools."[4] Brewer's family included several children, one of
whom was of school age. He was deeply troubled by the school
board's desegregation act, and after hearing a speech given by
an outspoken young segregationist named James Johnson,
Brewer began organizing the Citizens Committee.[5] The group
held a meeting on the night of August 3 in the Hoxie City Hall;
they discussed boycotting the school, planned to circulate petitions, and criticized the school board. Similar meetings during
the rest of August had larger and larger turnouts. Initially, the
committee apparently involved only local people, but as resis-

tance increased notable Arkansas segregationists such as Amis Guthridge and Johnson became active in the community.[6] These outsiders brought in segregationists from Mississippi and elsewhere, and Guthridge became the lawyer for Brewer's group.[7]

Even though the segregationists said their resistance would remain within the law, their actions were often inconsistent with that claim. Emotions rose as the school board stood by its decision and as segregationists resorted to systematic intimidation. Anonymous late-night phone calls, knocks on doors, and a boycott were part of the resistance effort.[8] At rallies inflammatory speeches were commonplace; threats were made repeatedly that "someone might get hurt" unless there were a return to separate schools. Guthridge at one point exclaimed that he could not be responsible if someone "should throw a rock through a car windshield and put out the eye" of a member of the school board. One segregationist speaker attacked the Fourteenth Amendment as a fraud, predicting that "blood would run knee-deep all over Arkansas" unless firearms and "grass ropes" were used to keep the "nigger out of the white bedroom." Lynching was a useful device for achieving such a purpose because the "power of government was with the people." Guthridge called the school board a tool of the Supreme Court's "revolutionary plot." He accused the Methodist Church of favoring integration and exclaimed that if anyone committed violence against a member of the school board, the FBI would be powerless to intervene. Johnson discussed the lynching of a black in Mississippi and predicted "mongrelization" of both white and black races if integration occurred.[9] Also singled out for attack were the University of Arkansas, Harry Ashmore, editor of the *Arkansas Gazette*, and Governor Orval E. Faubus.

Segregationists attacked Faubus because he refused to take a stand on the situation in Hoxie or on integration in general. "Whatever could be done might only aggravate the situation," he said in August, noting the presence of "out-of-Arkansas" influences.[10] Guthridge threatened that Faubus's refusal to become involved would lead to political opposition in the 1956 gubernatorial primary campaign. "Pretty soon we're going to tell Faubus he's either for white folks or for the NAACP, and we don't want any smart remarks."[11]

Segregationists had other strategies. Members of the Hoxie

Citizens Committee visited the homes of members of the school board and parents of black children. One such visit took place after midnight in an isolated rural area; although the visitors were not aggressive, the implications were ominous. An elderly father received an anonymous letter threatening that unless his seventeen-year-old son left the Hoxie school the youth would suffer the same fate as a black man lynched in Mississippi. For protection the father sent his son to Washington state. The pressure became so threatening that Hoxie's mayor, who regularly attended segregationist rallies, advised the school board to post guards at the school, which made sense because Guthridge and others trespassed on school property to "see how effectively their boycott was operating."[12]

The harassment campaign produced mixed results. The boycott reduced attendance in Hoxie's school by more than half, and only a handful of black children remained by the fall. Unable to endure persistent threats, the school board began the harvest recess on August 10, two weeks earlier than scheduled. At the same time, the board initiated a suit in federal court to determine the legality of the segregationists' claims that the voluntary desegregation of the Hoxie school district was contrary to the laws and constitution of Arkansas. The segregationists also began litigation of their own in state court, alleging financial irregularities on the part of members of the school board. After some procedural maneuvering, this suit brought to light a few questionable expenditures, but the court found that they did not justify criminal prosecution or involve civil liability. The decision did result in the resignation of at least one board member and the election of Brewer to replace him; but the majority of the school board continued to support desegregation.[13]

These developments complicated matters further. As tension mounted in the fall, United States Attorney General Herbert Brownell ordered an FBI investigation in Hoxie, which was perhaps the first time the Justice Department became directly involved in a desegregation suit. Both undercover and plain clothes agents went into the area, listening to and interviewing residents and uncovering solid evidence of segregationist harassment. Brownell's action, however, raised the threat of "foreign" federal intervention in the minds of some local people, and segregationists used it to justify their own conduct. At one rally FBI agents were identified in the crowd and Johnson gave a rousing speech attacking the attorney general and the Justice Department for threatening the constitutional rights of the community's citizens.[14]

On October 14 federal district judge Thomas C. Trimble in Little Rock issued a temporary restraining order forbidding segregationist interference with the operation of the Hoxie school. Segregationist attorneys attempted to block the order by challenging the federal court's jurisdiction. Trimble postponed a full hearing of the controversy to determine this jurisdictional question, but left his order in effect.[15] The school board then reopened the town's school on schedule after the harvest recess on October 24. By the end of the month Judge Trimble established his court's jurisdiction and exclaimed that the "court is trying to protect that community. Things in this case show it will soon develop into a riot."[16]

Issuing a temporary injunction, Trimble held that Guthridge, Brewer, and others had "planned and conspired" to prevent integration in Hoxie. The injunction stated that "defendants have committed and continued to commit and threaten acts of intimidation, coercion and boycott which interfere with the lawful operation of the Hoxie schools."[17] Trimble ruled further that Arkansas had no valid laws requiring racial segregation in public schools. A formal hearing was set for December to ascertain whether to make the injunction permanent; federal judge Albert L. Reeves was called out of retirement to preside. Evidence produced at the hearing established irrefutably the degree and impact of segregationist activities. On the basis of this proof Reeves made the injunction permanent, finding that "the defendants were attempting to substitute their own wills in lieu of the law . . . thereby depriving . . . [the Hoxie school district] of a representative government" and the black children of the district of their "rights and privileges."[18] Brewer appealed to the U.S. Circuit Court in St. Louis, but the judges there upheld Reeves on every point.[19]

Inherent in the resolution of the Hoxie controversy were several larger implications. Segregationists had established a state-

wide organization with interstate connections capable of force-
ful resistance based on states' rights and systematic harassment. A majority of locally elected school officials might be able
to preserve voluntary integration and stand up to this intimidation if assisted by the federal courts. Involvement by state
authorities, particularly the governor's office, was unnecessary
as long as the governor remained uncommitted on the desegregation issue. The Justice Department and the FBI could serve
a useful function, but unless the evidence they gathered was
used to prosecute wrongdoers such a role could do more harm
than good because segregationists could exploit local fears of
outsiders and foreigners. But perhaps the most significant result of the Hoxie controversy was that it catapulted into prom-
inence the vigorous and imaginative segregationist leader James
Johnson.

JOHNSON'S STRATEGY

Johnson was from Crossett, a town in southeastern Arkansas
just a few miles from the Louisiana border. While still in his
twenties the attorney was elected to the state senate, where he
was identified as an agrarian radical and defender of working
people's interests. Political observers characterized him as
handsome, personable, and an effective speaker with a reviv-
alist style and a willingness to cast himself as the underdog. In
1952 Johnson had campaigned for Francis Cherry in fifteen
counties in southern and eastern Arkansas. He was credited with
helping Cherry carry this region, which contributed to his election as governor. Despite his ability to garner the support of
his own "friends and neighbors," however, he was unable to
win in a state-wide race for attorney general in 1954.[20] The Supreme Court's Brown decision gave Johnson a new issue, which
he viewed in the same light as did his friend Senator James
Eastland of Mississippi, one of the South's most prominent and
vocal advocates of massive resistance to desegregation. Johnson's fervent advocacy of Eastland's defiant approach during the
Hoxie conflict brought the young lawyer considerable publicity, which in turn fueled speculation that he would become a
gubernatorial candidate in the 1956 summer primary.[21]

A Little Rock political commentator suggested something of

the ambivalence in Johnson's character and style. He was "a clever young attorney whose political ambitions have him running forward at such a reckless speed that he doesn't pause long enough to survey his possibilities, or to study the questions of whether his arguments are acceptable to the voters." There was no doubt, the commentator continued, that this "man has developed a fine oratory and probably could go places in the political field if his views were a little more rational and not so emotional." On television "he made an impressive appearance. But voters became afraid of his philosophy." Off the campaign trail in private discussions, however, Johnson displayed sound judgment and conveyed a sincere conviction that he was expressing the hopes, doubts, and fears of many whites who were too timid to speak out for themselves.[22]

The segregationist's public pronouncements reflect this ambivalence. He could state positively: "If you inform a Southern white person you will keep down a lot of violence. . . . If he knows his neighbors feel as he does, he will associate with them in settling their problems in a peaceful way." Then, more stridently, he could exclaim, "Arkansas people didn't start integration, but Arkansas people are going to stop it in Arkansas."[23] On other occasions Johnson affirmed that white citizens' groups espoused a "middle of the road" policy. Unlike those who wanted to settle the integration issue with "Old Betsy" (a shotgun), or others who advocated immediate integration, his people sought to maintain segregation through legal means.[24]

In keeping with his populist style, the lawyer understood desegregation in conspiratorial terms. In a letter to Senator Eastland, Johnson interpreted U.S. Supreme Court cases ordering integration of golf courses and other public recreational facilities as an indication of the Court's intention "to rule against states' rights to ban intermarriage of whites and non-whites." Johnson then noted that the decisions were handed down "on the day that Russia was celebrating a holiday commemorating the advent of communism in that country." The two events "may be coincidental," he concluded, "but it deserves the prayerful investigation of the U.S. Senate." If "ties are found to exist between the two, immediate impeachment proceedings should be commenced."[25]

As the trouble in Hoxie and Johnson's political chances attracted growing publicity, segregationists announced a political program aimed at either controlling or abolishing Arkansas public schools.[26] Rooted in racial feelings but fashioned and publicized in terms of states' rights, the program centered on passage of a state law that would authorize local school districts to "assign" white and black children to separate schools. However, if this effort failed, Guthridge said, resistance must be carried "even to the point of destroying the public school system" by electing school board members who would "reduce the millage rates to nothing . . . [and thereby destroy the] public status of the schools, permitting the buildings to be rented, leased or sold to private corporations to operate."[27]

The theory underlying this program was interposition, which would be implemented through a constitutional amendment. After the *Brown II* decision was handed down in June 1955, L. D. Poynter, president of White America, said that if segregationists could not get satisfaction from the state legislature they would "try to get . . . [the] state constitution amended to forestall action [on] integration." In August, in a meeting in Little Rock, anti-integration forces called for a constitutional amendment requiring segregation.[28] But by the fall, as it became clear that desegregation would continue in Hoxie, demand for constitutional action and the interposition principle underlying it were primarily identified with Johnson. The young activist had first learned of interposition from editorials written in 1954 by James J. Kilpatrick in the Richmond *News Leader*, editorials which "made sense" to the Arkansan.[29] Perhaps, too, Senator Eastland's use of interposition to justify "massive resistance" against *Brown* influenced Johnson.[30]

On November 15 Johnson announced at a rally that the "best legal minds in the South will meet soon in East Arkansas to draft a constitutional amendment to circumvent the U.S. Supreme Court integration ruling." Two weeks later he said that a "final draft" was "about ready" which contained the "best provisions" of similar amendments adopted in other southern states. Johnson's measure was published and circulated in a magazine he edited called *Arkansas Faith*.[31]

The proposal became known as the Johnson Amendment. It directed the Arkansas general assembly, scheduled to meet in

January 1957, to "take appropriate action and pass laws" whose
purpose was the "evasion" of *Brown* and subjected state officials to possible criminal prosecution if they failed to carry out
such laws. Once approved by the attorney general, the proposal would appear on the November 1956 ballot through the
state's initiative procedure, which required the signatures of a
certain percentage of Arkansas's voters. (The percentage of signatures necessary for an initiative act was 8 percent; a referendum required 6 percent and a constitutional amendment on the
ballot needed 10 percent—these percentages were based on voter
turnouts in the last gubernatorial election.) Johnson was confi-
dent of getting enough signatures because the amendment would
"absolutely guarantee continued segregation in the public schools
of Arkansas and in other phases of Arkansas society." After more
than 86,000 citizens signed their names, the attorney general
announced that the Johnson Amendment would be on the ballot for voter consideration in the fall.[32]

Johnson's possible gubernatorial aspirations aside, his spon-
sorship of the constitutional amendment was grounded in as-
sumptions and values that transcended political ambition.
Johnson was convinced that the roots of *Brown* lay in President
Harry S. Truman's campaign for reelection in 1948, and that
Truman, needing every bloc of votes he could get, desperately
raised the civil rights issue to get the support of blacks. The Supreme Court's overruling of the separate-but-equal doctrine,
Johnson believed, grew out of Truman's political opportunism.
Thus politics, not egalitarian idealism, explained *Brown*, eradi-
cating any basis the decision might have had in moral principle.[33]

Johnson saw the *Brown* decision as part of a larger usurpation of power. To the segregationist attorney, reverence toward
judges was vital to the perpetuation of representative government, because judges stabilized society by maintaining a "government of laws and not of men." But the Supreme Court's judicial activism, with integration being its most dangerous result,
undermined the judges' status, which in turn generated disorder. Considered in these terms, integration was not only unfair
to white southerners because they had lived for more than fifty
years under the constitutionality of segregation; it threatened

the very foundations of American government. And the Court had compounded the error by basing its reversal of the separate-but-equal doctrine on sociological writings of foreign writers such as Gunnar Myrdal, revealing the extent to which the federal judicial system was being used in "unorthodox ways."[34]

Johnson was also certain that the Court's action in *Brown* was unconstitutional. The decision, he said, fostered "encroachments upon rights and powers not delegated to the United States . . . by the Constitution"—and therefore violated the Tenth Amendment. Furthermore, the phrase "with all deliberate speed" in *Brown II* was "gutless," since something was either constitutional or it was not; it could not become "gradually constitutional." In these terms the lawyer answered moderates who, though disagreeing with *Brown*, would comply with the decision because it was the law of the land. For the outspoken segregationist the U.S. Constitution and acts of Congress passed in pursuance of it were the law of the land; the Court could do no more than interpret the Constitution and the laws. Johnson singled out the *Arkansas Gazette* and its editor, Harry Ashmore, as leading defenders of the moderate position. To Johnson this position defended a usurpation of congressional authority and a flouting of the Constitution that was more distressing than the social change being called for under the Court's desegregation decisions.[35]

In addition to his constitutional arguments, Johnson advocated a type of civil disobedience. It seemed reasonable to him that the surest way to defeat the *Brown* decision was to have it enforced vigorously, which would cause great public opposition. Since there were "not enough jails to punish all resisters," the clamor would force Congress to respond with legislation that either enforced segregation or declared it illegal. The interposition amendment was intended to demonstrate popular disagreement with *Brown* and thereby induce Congress to act. Johnson felt sure that Congress would not sanction integration; but if Congress did the unthinkable, he assumed that segregationists would comply.[36]

But Johnson advocated interposition for other reasons as well. He and fellow segregationists were particularly worried about the impact of integration in counties (such as those of East Arkansas) where blacks outnumbered whites. This imbalance created "population pressure" that would threaten all public education. Places such as Hoxie, while not actually located in the Delta, might serve as precedents for integrating schools in East Arkansas and elsewhere, and such precedents gave incentive to the NAACP to become active in an area.[37] The NAACP had begun operating in several Delta communities, and had already sounded out black support in Hoxie by the time Johnson started his constitutional amendment campaign.[38] These were the perceptions behind Johnson's formulation of the interposition issue in Arkansas.

Despite an underlying concern with race relations, the doctrine of interposition deflected attention away from questions of moral principle and equal justice, emphasizing instead a legalistic abstraction. But the legalism had symbolic and political force because Arkansans yearned to believe that there was some constitutional means to avoid desegregation. Resentment over the intervention of a "foreign" Supreme Court heightened the emotional appeal of the doctrine.[39]

Compounding these problems was the general view among American jurists and government officials that interposition lacked any legal or constitutional authority, as noted by Professor Robert A. Leflar of the University of Arkansas School of Law, one of the nation's foremost legal scholars and the leading jurisprudential thinker in the state. In his opinion, there was "no legal basis whatever" for the interposition theory "as a nullifying or voiding device. As anything more than a formal and official protest against federal action, the doctrine is a legal absurdity." As for assertions regarding the power of the Supreme Court, Leflar answered that there was in "our federalism" no "higher *judicial* authority" with "respect to the validity or invalidity of any governmental . . . action, state or federal, under the U.S. Constitution."[40]

Underlying these jurisprudential considerations, however, were the practical ramifications of interposition as a political issue, and perhaps no one perceived those political implications more clearly than Governor Faubus.

FAUBUS'S RESPONSE

Throughout his first year in office Faubus avoided direct involvement with desegregation. During the legislative session of 1955 he remained aloof from the debate over the segregationist measures that eventually failed to become law. Despite criticism from Guthridge and others, the governor refused to intervene in Hoxie.[41] He also condoned the desegregation of all Arkansas's public universities and colleges. But public acquiescence in desegregation did not mean that Faubus was unaware of the growing popular clamor arising from the issue, especially as it related to Johnson's possible gubernatorial candidacy in the 1956 summer Democratic primary.[42]

Faubus had long been aware of the difficulties desegregation created for those seeking elected office. In his race against Governor Cherry in 1954 he had introduced the issue, calling it the "number one" question in the campaign. At one point he pledged that if elected governor, his door would be open to all blacks, promising them employment in state government positions. Faubus cautioned, however, that he could "not pledge . . . that the children of both races will be completely mixed in all the public schools next year [1955], because knowing the problem of Arkansas as I do, I know it would be impossible for anyone to fulfill such a pledge." An editorial in the *Arkansas Gazette* condemned the reference to desegregation, and the candidate did not raise the subject again in the campaign. Cherry's effort to stigmatize Faubus as a Communist because he had attended Commonwealth College, an institution having that affiliation, probably drew attention away from the issue.[43]

After his election the new governor maintained a cautious position. There had been no mention of desegregation in Faubus's inaugural address in February 1955.[44] After the decision of *Brown II* in the spring, the governor expressed relief that the Court had "recognized the local nature of the problem," and observed that the "best solution" could be achieved on the "local level according to the peculiar circumstances of each school district." He welcomed, too, the supervisory role of the federal district court, which would "guarantee against any sudden dislocations." Nonetheless, Faubus stressed that the "new legal precedent" could "pose serious social problems in many communities of the state. Our reliance now must be upon the good will that exists between the two races—the good will that has long made Arkansas a model for other Southern states."[45]

Behind his caution was the practical awareness that any explicit endorsement of the desegregation principle itself could be politically disastrous. Faubus expressed such a view during a visit with the Arkansas congressional delegation in Washington, D.C., in early 1956, when most southern senators and congressmen were studying and preparing the Southern Manifesto, which condemned the Supreme Court and criticized *Brown* as unconstitutional. When asked what impact not signing would have on an official's chances for reelection, Faubus responded that he believed that most of the members of the delegation would go down to defeat unless they put their names on the manifesto.[46] This assessment seemed to be confirmed when a political unknown, campaigning on a segregationist platform, defeated by a 3 to 1 margin Alabama's populist governor, James Folsom, in a race for the Democratic Naional Committee. Faubus's perception was reinforced as he watched events unfold in several Texas and Kentucky communities as they struggled with desegregation.[47] Compounding further the political difficulties of state and local officials was President Dwight D. Eisenhower's refusal to take a strong stand favoring federal responsibility for enforcement of *Brown*. Eisenhower's position placed these authorities in the difficult (and to Faubus, unfair) position of having to confront a problem that was not of their making. The president's inaction meant that southern officials were faced with voter disapproval if they mishandled desegregation.[48]

But for Faubus desegregation as a political problem possessed a larger dimension involving the need to improve social and economic conditions in Arkansas. His commitment to reversing the state's history of backwardness placed Faubus in a southern political tradition known as neo-populism.[49] Early in his first term he became noted as Arkansas's best "welfare governor"; he increased welfare payments, decreased utility rates, improved social programs, enlarged state aid to education, and developed industry. Greater success was limited, however, by the failure, in the 1955 legislative session, of a Faubus-spon-

sored tax increase which would have provided fiscal support
for an even broader based program of social services and development. Faubus hoped for another opportunity to push for
a similar tax program in the assembly session of 1957; but the
chance for victory there depended upon being nominated and
then reelected in 1956. Traditionally, Arkansas governors encountered little opposition in the bid for a second term. But with
the emergence of the struggle in Hoxie and the possible candidacy of Johnson, Faubus perceived that his dreams for Arkansas and his own political future were seriously threatened.[50]

Other political factors heightened the governor's sensitivity
to the desegregation question. County interests dominated Arkansas politics to such an extent that, even though recognized
as one of the nation's "purest" one-party states, on any given
political issue there could be as many factions as there were
counties. In such a system local leaders possessed significant
power and influence. In his hard-fought victory over Cherry in
1954, Faubus received local support in the northern and western counties, but not in the Delta region of East Arkansas. After
his election Faubus sought to remedy this situation by appoint-
ing (or reappointing) East Arkansas local leaders to state offices
and by funneling patronage their way.[51]

Despite their preference for segregation, some local leaders
in the Delta were suspicious of the crusade of the white citizens' councils. To these leaders individuals like Johnson, Guthridge, and Brewer represented a challenge to the traditional basis of local control and authority, which depended upon
dominant influence over black voters. This influence was essential to the perpetuation of East Arkansas's political clout and
no doubt explained, at least in part, a Lincoln County sheriff's
suspicion of segregationists. "We're getting along fine without
any body stirring up trouble," he said.[52] As long as Faubus
wanted the support of Delta politicos, he could not afford to
take a desegregation stand that threatened the local power
structure.[53]

And there was yet another reason why Governor Faubus
needed the East Arkansas leadership on his side. In order for
a tax increase to get through the assembly, grass-roots support

across the state was essential. From the defeat in the legislative session of 1955, Faubus learned that urban centers such as Little Rock, areas bordering on states with low taxes, and even a few representatives in his own northwestern part of the state would oppose increased taxes—even if he were reelected to sponsor them in 1957. There would be enough votes among counties in the rest of the state for passage of a tax package only if Delta representatives supported the governor.[54]

These considerations no doubt influenced two of Faubus's early administrative appointments. He selected J. L. (Bex) Shaver, a leading lawyer and political figure in Cross County, as legislative secretary. Shaver had served his county, which was located just across the Mississippi River from Memphis, for fourteen years in the assembly, had been a two-term lieutenant governor, and was active in the state bar association, having at one time been president. As a prominent attorney, Shaver devoted part of his practice to working with black clients, sometimes without fee.[55] The governor also drew upon East Arkansas leadership in reappointing as chairman of the state board of education Marvin E. Bird of Crittenden County. More than half of the funds from any tax increase would be used for education, and the state board chairman would have a key role in administering the expenditures.[56]

During 1955 Faubus formed a cooperative relationship with those East Arkansas interests that seemed unaffected by his lack of support for the Delta-sponsored segregation measures defeated early in the assembly session of 1955. Perhaps cooperation developed despite the governor's noncommitment because the legislation was relatively moderate, consistent with the view toward desegregation that R. B. McCulloch had presented in the Arkansas brief for *Brown II*.[57] Once the Supreme Court affirmed the moderate position, failure of the legislation may have seemed less pressing. Also, the measures had come up before a die-hard segregationist threat to local leaders, represented by Johnson and others, had emerged out of the Hoxie struggles.[58] Faubus's skill in using state appointments to gain the favor of such influential leaders as Shaver and Bird was undoubtedly another factor in diluting any ill-will concerning the legislation of 1955. But during early 1956, as winter turned into spring and the time for filing for the Democratic primary neared, Faubus found that unless he took a firm stand on interposition his local support in the Delta and across Arkansas was in jeopardy.

THE GUBERNATORIAL CAMPAIGN OF 1956

Faubus became increasingly concerned about the segregationists' grass-roots strength. Local contacts throughout the state discovered that Johnson's growing influence threatened the governor's political standing. Faubus asked his pollster to sample opinion in several counties, especially those in southern and east-central Arkansas where Johnson was considered most attractive to voters. The poll confirmed the strength of anti-integration feeling, especially in rural areas, and demonstrated that Johnson was the candidate to beat.[59] Late in January 1956 Faubus announced that his poll showed that about 85 percent of Arkansans opposed racially integrated schools and said that if complete integration ever came to the state it would be "a slow process." The governor declared that a "court edict" could not change "centuries old customs" and that he could not "be a party to any attempt to force acceptance of change to which the people are so overwhelmingly opposed."[60]

Public announcement of the poll results was part of a well-conceived approach to interposition. Faubus had initially considered the states' rights theory impractical because the federal government possessed greater power than the states; the idea of an "interposing" state authority therefore seemed hollow. As the campaign for the Johnson Amendment gained political force, however, Governor Faubus realized that he could not remain silent on the issue. Political considerations also influenced whom he chose to formulate his interposition stand: he turned for guidance to East Arkansas local leaders.[61] Faubus formed a committee chaired by Marvin Bird which included Shaver, McCulloch, and two others: B. G. Dickey, a planter-businessman from the Delta community of West Memphis, and Charles T. Adams, also from the region, and a member of the state game and fish commission. Faubus charged the Bird Committee to develop a set of interposition recommendations that would enable Arkansas to comply with *Brown II*, but that would also preserve the symbolic appeal of states' rights. A central focus of the committee's work was the program of interposition formulated in Virginia. From college days Shaver had known the man responsible for key measures of the Old Dominion program, William Tuck. After visiting Virginia and comparing Tuck's proposals with the more radical laws of Georgia, the Bird Committee based its recommendations on the more moderate approach.[62]

Shaver's views concerning desegregation suggested the values underlying the Bird Committee's recommendations. The lawyer did not question the Supreme Court's authority to decide *Brown*; the constitutional power behind the decision was no different from that behind the handing down of the separate-but-equal doctrine more than a half century earlier. To Shaver both decisions involved a "sociological" purpose, but *Brown* raised the hard political problem of creating public support among people who largely disagreed with desegregation. Shaver acknowledged that racial justice was a "truth" worth working for, but he was also acutely conscious of the difficulty of changing people's thinking.[63]

Contrary to the defiant nature of Georgia's laws and the Johnson Amendment, Shaver believed that interposition—properly conceived—could facilitate a change in thought "from the ground up." "Fear of coercion from Federal authorities and fear of being forced to do something against the overwhelming sentiment of the people" of Arkansas, Shaver observed, create "uneasiness and discontent and result in extreme views and attitudes." Achievement of "social justice" might take a "long time," for it is not something that can be "legislated"; it has "to come from the hearts of the people. When you compel people to do what they do not believe in their hearts is right, it will take the power of a police state . . . to carry it out. Real progress wells from the people and is not handed down from above."[64]

What form could interposition proposals take to achieve these purposes? The first recommendation of the Bird Committee was a measure designed only to determine the opinion of voters regarding desegregation; copied from the Virginia resolutions, it contained high-sounding states' rights phrases but offered no

concrete course of action or use of state power to prevent the
enforcement of *Brown*.[65] McCulloch termed the proposal nothing more than a resolution, "not an amendment, not even a
law."[66] The committee's second recommendation was a pupil
assignment measure that stipulated eighteen factors (excluding
race) that could be used to assign students to schools. Following the approach taken in his *Brown II* brief, McCulloch drafted
the proposal so that it conformed to laws already sustained by
the federal courts.[67]

As the Bird Committee did its work early in 1956, Faubus came
under mounting segregationist pressure. Johnson, who had already filed to have his interposition amendment appear on the
fall ballot, urged the governor to call a special session of the
state assembly to consider anti-integration legislation. Shortly
thereafter (suggesting Johnson's growing influence in the Delta)
an East Arkansas assemblyman circulated petitions requesting
a special session. Faubus refused to accede to these demands
and countered by announcing the activities of the Bird Committee.[68] Following this announcement, the *Southern School News*
ran the headline "Governor of Arkansas Inclines to Segregation." Characteristically, however, Faubus phrased his endorsement of interposition cautiously, noting the extent to which
desegregation was a "local problem . . . best . . . solved on
the local level according to the peculiar circumstances and conditions of each local school district."[69] This position tacitly
sanctioned desegregation where it had already occurred, in
places like Hoxie and northwestern Arkansas, which permitted
Faubus to identify himself as a moderate compared to unequivocal segregationists like Johnson.[70] Shunning an extremist image, the governor could plead for "the cooperation of all the
people in upholding law and order and in preserving . . . peace
and harmony."[71]

Interposition soon became the central issue in the gubernatorial primary race of 1956. In late April Johnson formally accepted a draft by segregationists to run for governor on an interposition platform. Faubus then became a candidate (along with
several others) and announced his acceptance of the Bird Committee's interposition resolution and pupil assignment provi-
sion. To facilitate the gathering of the petition signatures necessary for placing the measures on the November ballot, Faubus

designated the governor's office as temporary headquarters for receiving and processing petitions. Having thus firmly established his position on interposition, the governor began campaigning in earnest for the nomination in the Democratic primary of July 31.[72]

During the campaign Johnson charged Faubus with "pussy-footing" on integration. The governor responded with an offer of state aid to school districts that decided to oppose desegregation in the courts. "No school district will be forced," he said, "to mix races as long as I am Governor."[73] At another point he exclaimed, "I am convinced that the surest way to safeguard our public school system at present for all citizens—both white and Negro—is to preserve our segregated schools."[74] Faubus did not, however, retreat from a position favoring desegregation as an issue that should be left to local choice. At the same time he repeatedly brought to the attention of voters his good record on improved social services and industrial development, which gained him the support of blacks.[75] Gradually the campaign became so heated that Faubus felt the need for a security guard, which apparently was necessary on at least one occasion.[76]

Arkansas voters reelected the governor in a landslide. Faubus received 180,760 votes to Johnson's 83,856, other candidates dividing among themselves some 45,000 votes. The county vote breakdown suggested that Faubus had been justified in his concern for the grass-roots appeal of the segregationist. Johnson carried seven counties in the southwestern and east-central part of the state, as well as Hoxie (though Faubus carried the county of which Hoxie was part). The vote for Johnson was the highest of any runner-up in a race against an incumbent governor in the state's recent history. Charging election fraud, the segregationist leader refused to concede defeat and formed a new states' rights party which would fight on for interposition.[77] As the summer of 1956 ended, however, Faubus had revealed unmatched skill in turning that issue to political advantage by maintaining the support of Arkansas's relatively moderate mainstream voters.

The politicization of the interposition issue made Faubus vulnerable to segregationist attacks. Presenting himself as a populist on development and a moderate on desegregation, Faubus gained a landslide victory in the gubernatorial primary of 1956, even receiving the votes of independent blacks in places like Little Rock. But although the governor's strategy seemed astute in the short run, in the long run it entangled him more deeply in the politics of symbolism and the rule of law. To protect the populism he so cherished, Faubus would now respond to the segregationists' interposition arguments with an increasingly aggressive states' rights stand. Johnson's formation of a party dedicated to overturning the *Brown* decisions assured that interposition would remain a live issue. Whether Governor Faubus could meet this challenge and still avoid capitulating to the hard-line segregationists became the central issue of Arkansas politics.

NOTES

1. Memo, Mildred L. Bond to Roy Wilkins, Aug. 6, 1955, DBP (SHSW, AD), MS. 523, Box 4. *SSN*, Aug. 1955, 15; Sept. 1955, 10; Oct. 1955, 10. J. W. Peltason, *Fifty-Eight Lonely Men: Southern Federal Judges and School Desegregation* (New York, 1961), 149–151. G. W. Foster, Jr., "Education and Law: Segregation in Public Schools" (manuscript, 1962), chap. 3, p. 7. Orval Eugene Faubus, *Down from the Hills* (Little Rock, 1980), 95, 100, 107, 114, 116, 117.

2. *SSN*, Aug. 1955, 15. For details concerning school structure and administration see memo, Bond to Wilkins, Aug. 6, 1955, and *SSN*, Aug. 1955.

3. See also "Finding of Fact and Conclusions of Law Proposed by Plaintiffs," *Aaron* v. *Cooper* Files, #1, NAACP LDF.

4. *SSN*, Aug. 1955, 15; "Finding of Fact," *Aaron* v. *Cooper* Files.

5. James S. Johnson, interview with author, Sept. 4, 1980.

6. Memo, Bond to Wilkins, Aug. 6, 1955.

7. "Finding of Fact," *Aaron* v. *Cooper* Files; Johnson interview, Sept. 4, 1980.

8. "Finding of Fact," *Aaron* v. *Cooper* Files; *Hoxie* v. *Brewer*, 1 *RRLR* 43 (U.S.D.C. E.D. Ark. 1955); *Hoxie* v. *Brewer*, 1 *RRLR* 299 (U.S.D.C. E.D. Ark. 1956); *Brewer* v. *Hoxie*, 1 *RRLR* 1027 (U.S.C.A. 8th Cir. 1956).

9. See note 8 above.

10. *SSN*, Sept. 1955, 10; Oct. 1955, 10.

11. *SSN*, Sept. 1955, 10.

12. See note 8 above.

13. Johnson interview, Sept. 4, 1980. Harry Ashmore to Tony Freyer, Apr. 21, 1981, June 2, 1981. Boyce Alexander Drummond, Jr., "Arkansas Politics: A Study of a One-Party System" (Ph.D. diss., University of Chicago, 1957), 144. Faubus, *Down from the Hills*, 144. See also *SSN*, Jan. 1956, 9; Feb. 1956, 11; Mar. 1956, 13; Apr. 1956, 9. For initial litigation see *Hoxie* v. *Brewer*, 1 *RRLR* 43 (1955).

14. *SSN*, Oct. 1955, 10; Nov. 1956, 12. "Finding of Fact," *Aaron* v. *Cooper* Files. Johnson interview, Sept. 4, 1980. Foster, "Education and Law," chap. 3, p. 7.

15. *Hoxie* v. *Brewer*, 1 *RRLR* 43 (1955).

16. *SSN*, Dec. 1955, 9; Nov. 1955, 3.

17. 1 *RRLR* 43, 45 (U.S.D.C. E.D. Ark. 1955). Johnson was not named in the injunction.

18. 1 *RRLR* 299, 304 (U.S.D.C. E.D. Ark. 1956). See also *SSN* citations in notes 13 and 14 above.

19. 1 *RRLR* 1027 (U.S.C.A. 8th Cir. 1956).

20. Johnson interview, Sept. 4, 1980. Ashmore to author, Apr. 21, 1981, June 2, 1981. Drummond, "Arkansas Politics," 144. Faubus, *Down from the Hills*, 144.

21. Johnson interview, Sept. 4, 1980. Faubus, *Down from the Hills*, 95, 100, 107, 114, 116, 117, 120–122. *SSN*, Sept. 1955, 10; Oct. 1955, 10; Nov. 1955, 3; Dec. 1955, 9. Numan V. Bartley, *The Rise of Massive Resistance: Race and Politics in the South during the 1950s* (Baton Rouge, 1969), 100, 101, 103.

22. George Douthit, *Arkansas Democrat* reporter for state politics and the capitol, as quoted in Faubus, *Down from the Hills*, 144. The last observation is based on Johnson interview, Sept. 4, 1980, and on his capable record as an associate justice of the Arkansas Supreme Court, 1958–1964.

23. *SSN*, Oct. 1955, 10.

24. Ibid., Dec. 1955, 9.

25. Ibid.

26. Ibid., Oct. 1955, 10. Faubus, *Down from the Hills*, 107, 114, 116, 117, 120–122.

27. *SSN*, Nov. 1955, 3.

28. Ibid., June 1955, 2; Sept. 1955, 10.

29. Johnson interview, Sept. 4, 1980. See also Virginius Dabney, *Across the Years: Memories of a Virginian* (Garden City, N.Y., 1978), 232–233; Bartley, *Massive Resistance*, 126–129.

30. For the Johnson-Eastland connection see *SSN*, Dec. 1955, 9; and Bartley, *Massive Resistance*, 119–120, 132.

31. *SSN*, Dec. 1955, 9; Jan. 1956, 9. For ambiguity and diversity in

interposition measures across the South, see Bartley, *Massive Resistance*, 126–149.

32. *SSN*, Feb. 1956, 2. See also *SSN*, Mar. 1956, 2; Apr. 1956, 8; June 1956, 9; Aug. 1956, 3; Johnson interview, Sept. 4, 1980; Bartley, *Massive Resistance*, 132; Faubus, *Down from the Hills*, 107, 114, 116, 117, 120–122.

33. Johnson interview, Sept. 4, 1980.

34. Ibid. Bartley, *Massive Resistance*, 126–149, especially 132, places Johnson's views in the context of development regarding interposition in the South in general.

35. *SSN*, Feb. 1956, 2; Mar. 1956, 2; Apr. 1956, 8; June 1956, 9; Aug. 1956, 3; Johnson interview, Sept. 4, 1980.

36. Johnson interview, Sept. 4, 1980.

37. Ibid.

38. "Parents' Petition, NAACP Authorization," DBP (SHSW, AD), MS. 523, Box 5. Memo, Bond to Wilkins, Aug. 6, 1955. Wiley A. Branton to H. R. Weaver, Sept. 30, 1955, DBP (SHSW, AD), MS. 523, Box 4.

39. On this point generally see Bartley, *Massive Resistance*, 126–149. See also Tony A. Freyer, "Politics and Law in the Little Rock Crisis, 1954–1957," *Arkansas Historical Quarterly*, 40 (Autumn 1981), 195–219.

40. *SSN*, Mar. 1956, 2. See also "Interposition vs. Judicial Power: A Study of Ultimate Authority in Constitutional Questions," 1 *RRLR* 465 (Dec. 1956).

41. *SSN*, Sept. 1955, 10; Oct. 1955, 10; see also discussion in chap. 1, 23, 24.

42. Faubus, *Down from the Hills*, 95, 100, 107, 114, 116, 117, 119–122, 124–125, 126–130.

43. "Faubus First to Inject Racial Issue (1954 gubernatorial race)," DBP (SHSW, AD), MS. 523, Box 5, File 10. Daisy Bates, *The Long Shadow of Little Rock, A Memoir* (New York, 1962), 48–49. Faubus, *Down from the Hills*, 24. *SSN*, Feb. 1955, 3.

44. *SSN*, Feb. 1955, 3.

45. *SSN*, June 1955, 2.

46. Faubus, *Down from the Hills*, 119–120, 129. See also Bartley, *Massive Resistance*, 116–117.

47. Faubus, *Down from the Hills*, 123, 128.

48. Ibid., 123. See also Bartley, *Massive Resistance*, 61–64.

49. Bartley, *Massive Resistance*, 20–21.

50. For Faubus's accomplishments and hopes for 1957, see Faubus, *Down from the Hills*, 97, 100, 101–107, 117–118, 124, 132, 133, 199. See also *SSN*, Feb. 1955, 2; Mar. 1955, 2.

51. Bartley, *Massive Resistance*, 101, 103. Drummond, "Arkansas Politics," 177–178. Faubus, *Down from the Hills*, 120–122.

52. *Arkansas Gazette*, Oct. 14, 1955, and chap. 1.

53. Bartley, *Massive Resistance*, 101, 103. Drummond, "Arkansas Politics," 177–178. Faubus, *Down from the Hills*, 120–122.

54. Orval Faubus, interview with author, July 15, 1980; Faubus, *Down from the Hills*, 167, 169.

55. J. L. (Bex) Shaver, interview with author, Aug. 15, 1980. Bartley, *Massive Resistance*, 101.

56. *SSN*, Jan. 1955, 3; Feb. 1955, 2. Bartley, *Massive Resistance*, 101.

57. *SSN*, Jan. 1955, 3; Feb. 1955, 2. Bartley, *Massive Resistance*, 101. See also chap. 1.

58. See discussion in chap. 1, 24, 35.

59. Faubus, *Down from the Hills*, 114, 120–123.

60. *SSN*, Feb. 1956, 1.

61. Faubus interview, July 15, 1980. See also Faubus, *Down from the Hills*, 95, 100, 107, 114, 116, 117, 119–122, 124–125, 126–130; and Bartley, *Massive Resistance*, 101.

62. Shaver interview, Aug. 15, 1980. *SSN*, Mar. 1956, 4. B. G. Dickey to Leon B. Catlett, Mar. 12, 1956, LBCF. Bartley, *Massive Resistance*, 109, 115. "Interim Report of Special Committee," Feb. 24, 1956, mimeograph, LBCF.

63. Shaver interview, Aug. 15, 1980.

64. *Civil Rights Hearings before Subcommittee No. 5 of the Committee on the Judiciary, House of Representatives, Eighty-Fifth Session* (Washington, D.C., 1957), 1188 (I am grateful to Mr. Shaver for use of his copy of the report). For other comments see Shaver interview, Aug. 15, 1980, and "Interim Report."

65. "Interim Report."

66. *SSN*, June 1956, 10.

67. Ibid. See also "Interim Report"; and Bartley, *Massive Resistance*, 131–132, 137, 141–144, 146, 147.

68. *SSN*, Mar. 1956, 4; Apr. 1956, 8. See also Faubus, *Down from the Hills*, 95, 100, 107, 114, 116, 117, 119–122, 124–125, 126–130.

69. *SSN*, Apr. 1956, 8.

70. Bartley, *Massive Resistance*, 142.

71. *SSN*, Apr. 1956, 8. Faubus, *Down from the Hills*, 120–122, 131, explains his motives in terms that coincide with Bartley's view on "relative" moderation.

72. *SSN*, Apr. 1956, 8; May 1956, 10; June 1956, 10; July 1956, 9; Aug. 1956, 3. See also Faubus, *Down from the Hills*, 130–141.

73. Faubus, *Down from the Hills*, 132, 135. See also citations in *SSN*, in note 72 above.

74. *SSN*, July 1956, 9.
75. See note 72 above.
76. Faubus, *Down from the Hills*, 138–141.
77. Ibid., 141, 145. Also see citations in *SSN* in note 72 above.

The Crisis Breaks ———— 4

American constitutional precedent and history to the contrary, states' rights doctrines became a powerful force in shaping the public attitudes upon which depended an orderly implementation of *Brown*. The interplay of politics, interposition, and the *Aaron* case fostered conflicting impressions of the Supreme Court's decision, generating uncertainty and confusion. In November 1956 voters would express their opinion on the interposition measures of Johnson and Faubus. Early in 1957 the Arkansas assembly would receive from the governor recommendations for increased taxes. And after a long summer a few black children in Little Rock were slated to enter Central High School on September 3. These and other events compelled Arkansas and Little Rock citizens and leaders to decide where they stood on integration and the constitutional authority behind it.

FAUBUS AND INTERPOSITION POLITICS, 1956–1957

The vote in the 1956 election demonstrated widespread popular doubt concerning the means of, and necessity for, complying with the *Brown* decisions. Johnson's Amendment 47 to the Arkansas constitution, aimed at nullifying the Court's decisions until Congress acted, passed by a vote of 185,374 to 146,064. The margin of support was even greater for the more moderate proposals sponsored by Faubus. The pupil assign-

ment law was approved 214,712 to 121,129, and the interposition resolution was approved 199,511 to 127,360. An indication
of the extent of white control of the black electorate in East Arkansas was the tally in Ward 4 of West Memphis. Voters in this
predominantly black community supported Amendment 47 by
a margin of 521 to 41, the interposition resolution by the same
margin, and the pupil assignment law by a vote of 545 to 17.[1]
The margins of voter approval were also significant in Little Rock.
In the Pulaski county wards, which largely encompassed the
capital city, Johnson's amendment passed 27,325 to 16,660, the
resolution of interposition 23,038 to 17,808, and the pupil assignment law 27,325 to 16,666.[2]

Shortly after the election Superintendent Blossom wrote to A.
F. House and Leon Catlett, seeking to learn whether the election results would interfere with the Little Rock school board's
desegregation program. Blossom particularly wanted to know
whether the states' rights measures might influence Judge Miller's order in the *Aaron* case and whether they would have a
bearing on the appeal of the *Aaron* case scheduled for decision
in the spring of 1957.[3] For himself and Catlett, House replied
that neither Amendment 47 nor the interposition resolution
should affect the integration plan. Even if the Arkansas legislature passed laws aimed at impeding or preventing judicially
sanctioned desegregation, they would have no constitutional or
legal authority. House noted that the pupil assignment law did
apply to all school districts throughout the state; but its immediate impact on Miller's court order was unclear. "In our opinion," House concluded, "no pupil assignment law can displace
federal court supervision. If, however, our conclusion proves
to be incorrect, at the appropriate time we should ask that the
supervision being given by Judge Miller be terminated."[4] Blossom's questions and House's response were published in the
Arkansas Democrat and the *Arkansas Gazette*.[5]

No doubt the lawyer's assessment of the impact of the states'
rights measures was correct as a matter of law. His analysis failed
to consider, however, that interposition had achieved a symbolic and political force by the end of 1956 that transcended the
logic of legal reasoning. Once interposition formally became part
of the state's law in November, legislators in the upcoming ses-

sion of 1957 were bound to consider a number of segregation measures.[6] One such proposal (a result of Amendment 47) would create a state sovereignty commission with extensive investigative and police powers. Newly elected state attorney general Bruce Bennett sponsored other legislation requiring supporters of desegregation, particularly local NAACP branches, to register and make public reports of their activities. And, finally, Governor Faubus pushed for his own enactments: one to relieve school children of compulsory attendance in racially mixed school districts, the other to authorize school districts to hire legal counsel to defend school boards and school officials in suits involving desegregation.[7] Although he had not sponsored them, Faubus publicly supported the Bennett and sovereignty commission measures, despite their doubtful constitutionality and threat to civil liberties.[8]

These proposals were the center of public attention when the assembly session began in February 1957. Winthrop Rockefeller (the governor's appointee to head the Arkansas Industrial Development Commission) was particularly critical of the state sovereignty commission proposal. The bill was "dangerous" and provided the means to establish an "Arkansas gestapo," Rockefeller contended; no organization "would be safe from embarrassment of an investigation, and behind closed doors, too."[9] In a private report the local NAACP concluded that the courts would almost certainly declare unconstitutional most or all of the sovereignty commission provisions, as well as the Bennett legislation. But such litigation could become drawn out, during which time state officials might cause considerable trouble for the equal rights organization.[10]

About nine hundred persons attended the hearings dealing with the segregationist measures. Supporters and opponents gave testimony. As he had in 1955, Little Rock Senator Max Howell attempted to kill the bills through parliamentary procedure. Bex Shaver and R. B. McCulloch blunted these efforts by arguing that the proposed legislation was essentially moderate and part of the move toward gradual desegregation in Arkansas.[11] Subsequently, all the anti-desegregation legislation (including that sponsored by Faubus) passed both houses by substantial majorities. In a public statement Faubus contended that the "fear of 'witch hunts' or serious jeopardy of the rights of any citizen [is], in my belief, unfounded." The laws would "protect the rights of the people as to the will of the majority." That the governor's support for the controversial proposals was not founded in a desire to attack civil liberties is suggested by his veto of a loyalty bill that also came out of the assembly session.[12]

Although the debate over the legislation was significant in and of itself, it also should be viewed in the context of private political maneuvering that had even larger implications. Along with these laws, the legislature was asked to vote on a $22 million tax program, which represented the largest tax increase in the state's history. The governor had developed the program during the fall of 1956 as the heart of his plan to improve social and economic conditions.[13]

To mobilize the support necessary for the tax increase, Faubus turned to Little Rock attorney William J. Smith. Smith replaced Shaver, who had become the governor's primary representative in desegregation matters. It was widely recognized that Smith was perhaps more experienced in the politics of legislative approval than anyone else in the state. He had worked closely with five Arkansas governors, including Ben Laney, in whose administration he had engineered what was to that time the state's largest increase in taxes. From the 1940s on Smith had been active in Arkansas's Young Democrats and had served on the state's Workmen's Compensation Board. The attorney's brother was a high-ranking manager for Dun & Bradstreet in New York. Smith's legal, political, and business connections suited the needs of the Faubus administration well. Prior to the governor's second-term gubernatorial race, Smith had had no contact with Faubus. Indeed, he had been personal counsel to Governor Cherry, whom Faubus had defeated in 1954. But in the fall of 1956, after a lengthy private exchange of views concerning Arkansas's future, Smith joined the governor's staff, becoming Faubus's closest advisor.[14]

In his second-term inaugural address Governor Faubus linked passage of the tax program to desegregation. The "problem" of "racial segregation," he said, had "upset and confused the en-

tire South." Southerners were not a "lawless people," but the
Supreme Court had sought to "wipe out generations of human
attitudes, traditions and customs." It was "folly . . . to expect
judicial dictation to compel social adjustment." The race problem, Faubus reasoned, was a "compelling reason for favorable
consideration of the tax program" because "if all our people are
given good service . . . there is less likelihood of discord and
disorder in dealing with this or any other problem."[15]

Although the public was unaware of it, the linkage of tax and
segregation measures became even more intimate during the
assembly session. In the first half of the session the legislature
considered the tax increase, passage of which was unlikely
without East Arkansas support. Under Smith's guidance the tax
program did pass, largely because the Delta legislators voted
for it. The assembly debated the East Arkansas-sponsored state
sovereignty commission during the second half of the session.
At the same time opponents of the tax increase introduced legislation to repeal the program that had just become law. In order to prevent this, Faubus privately agreed to put his influence behind the sovereignty commission bill in return for
continued support from the Delta. The governor later wrote that
once the region's delegation sided with him on the tax legislation "I could not . . . ignore them."[16]

Entangling the fate of the neo-populist developmental program with interposition politics had ominous implications. Rec-
ognizing the impressive skill and organization responsible for
the tax victory, some political observers speculated that the
governor might be able to overcome tradition and be elected to
a third term. Publicly, at least, Faubus was noncommittal on the
question, but the private agreement involving East Arkansas
votes, defense of the sovereignty commission bill, acquiescence
in Bennett's laws, and sponsorship of his own anti-desegregation measures tied the governor's prestige and influence—and
thus his political future—to some form of continued segregation.[17] Furthermore, Faubus's actions undermined the persuasiveness of constitutional and legal arguments set forth in the
Blossom-House letters, published in the fall of 1956, which were
aimed at countering Guthridge's claims that Little Rock's de-

segregation program was contrary to states' rights and therefore invalid. All this could not help but encourage segregationists to stir up more trouble.

MOUNTING TENSIONS AND SECRET MANEUVERS

In March 1957 Little Rock school officials confronted a direct
segregationist challenge. Two positions on the school board
opened up, requiring a city-wide election. A dentist, George P.
Branscum, chairman of a states' rights organization known as
the Constitution Party, and Robert Ewing Brown, a radio and
television executive who was secretary-treasurer of the party and
president of the Capital Citizens' Council, sought election on
the basis of segregationist principles. Wayne Upton, a lawyer,
and Henry V. Rath, a businessman, ran as moderates who accepted the need to comply with federal court orders involving
desegregation.[18] Branscum and Brown, with the support of the
Save Our Schools Committee, focused their campaign on the
city's moderate-income, working-class voting wards where parents and children would be the first to experience desegregation at Central High. Principal support for the moderates came
from upper-income Pulaski Heights and Little Rock's primarily
black residential areas. Segregationists pushed a strong states'
rights, class-oriented campaign in the working-class neighborhoods, whose voters outnumbered those in high-income and
black wards. These efforts produced only a low turnout however, which meant that whites in Pulaski Heights and blacks
were able to give the moderates a substantial victory.[19] Upton
defeated Brown 4,340 to 2,398 and Rath won over Branscum
4,267 to 2,455.[20]

In April the school board gained another victory, this time in
court. After Judge Miller's decision upheld the Phase Program
in *Aaron* v. *Cooper* in August 1956, the NAACP had appealed to
the U.S. Court of Appeals in St. Louis. The NAACP considered
the case significant enough that Thurgood Marshall, chief counsel
for the Legal Defense Fund, joined Wiley Branton in oral arguments, but Miller's opinion was sustained. NAACP attor-

neys gave no indication as to whether they would make one last appeal to the U.S. Supreme Court.[21]

Neither of these victories, however, reduced the school board's uneasiness over mounting segregationist pressure. During preparation of briefs in the *Aaron* appeal House wrote to Catlett, "In view of what the Legislature is doing [in passing the various segregation measures] you should be prepared to explain to the Court how there can be an island of constitutionality in a sea of lawlessness."[22] As had occurred in *Hoxie*, Guthridge gave substance to such concerns by exclaiming that "there will never be integration in Little Rock in public schools," but if it did come in September, there would be "Hell on the border." Brown predicted "considerable and continuing protests against race mixing." Blacks had "ample and fine schools" in Little Rock, but trouble arose, he concluded, due to "the aims of a few white and Negro revolutionaries in the local Urban League and the National Association for the Advancement of Colored People."[23] Perhaps because of the injunction imposed in the *Hoxie* case, Guthridge and other local segregationists repeatedly affirmed a commitment to lawful implementation of their goals, but assertions by some advocates raised doubts about the depth of this commitment. At one meeting of the Capital Citizens' Council a guest speaker from Dallas, Texas, Rev. J. A. Lovell, stated that if the Supreme Court and elected officials kept "their weak-kneed" attitude toward integration "there are people left yet in the South who love God and their nation enough to shed blood if necessary to stop this work of Satan."[24]

In late June and early July the Capital Citizens' Council directly challenged the school board to alter its desegregation program. Representing a group of white parents whose children would attend Central High School in September, Guthridge appeared before the board to present the case for the childrens' "rights." The attorney claimed that the Supreme Court had not ordered "compulsory integration" in *Brown*, and urged the board to provide white children with segregated schools (which the CCC would pay for). Guthridge argued that certain state laws provided the means to establish these schools, and then he asked a number of questions concerning possible inter-

racial "social mingling" at school activities. On July 11 Guthridge wrote and published a letter summarizing his clients' case
and concluding that the board's program allowed black children to choose their school, but "trapped" white children by
forcing them to attend Central.[25]

States' rights abstractions aside, Guthridge's argument was
not without substance. Under the Blossom Plan Hall High was
slated to open as a totally white school, but school officials
probably could have found a basis in the state's new pupil assignment law to transfer children of dissatisfied white parents
in Central's district to Hall. Certainly there had been little difficulty in using transfer provisions in the Blossom Plan to reduce to a mere handful the number of blacks eligible to attend
Central. The refusal to desegregate Hall seemed to substantiate
segregationists' claims that "blue stocking" residents of Pulaski
Heights were being favored over the "common people."[26]

The school board replied to Guthridge's letter in a published
statement. The board repeated its general disagreement with
Brown, but reasserted a determination to comply with the law.
It also noted the unlikelihood of interracial mixing in the school's
social activities. Primarily, however, the statement attempted to
counter claims that state law could remove the obligation to obey
a federal court order. Reference was made to Article VI of the
Constitution, which made that document and laws "made in
pursuance thereof . . . the supreme law of the land . . . the
Constitution or laws of any State to the contrary notwithstand-
ing." To Little Rock school officials the language was "unmis-
takable and those who say State laws permitting segregation,
directly or indirectly, are supreme simply refuse to read that
which is plainly written." The statement pointed out further that
two federal courts had upheld the Phase Program. The school
board then invited CCC officials to test their arguments by litigating the Blossom Plan in court, which was the "traditional
American way" of settling conflicts between state and federal
authority. Until segregationists pursued this means of redress
the board urged an end to "insinuations" that it was cooperat-
ing with the NAACP or that the desegregation program was
illegal under state law.[27]

Underlying the board's statement was growing concern over

segregationist pressure. Superintendent Blossom sent his daughter to stay with relatives who lived in another part of Arkansas and began making periodic calls to Little Rock police authorities to learn of any racially connected disturbances. Blossom also established, by phone and through visits, regular contact with Governor Faubus.[28]

But the strongest action occurred early in June 1957 when A. F. House went to Washington, D.C., to talk with Arkansas native Arthur B. Caldwell, an attorney in the Justice Department and head of the Civil Rights Section. Speaking for the board, House sought to alert the department to the rising segregationist clamor. Caldwell came to Little Rock and met privately with House, Blossom, Ashmore (editor of the *Arkansas Gazette*), Police Chief Marvin H. Potts, and Judge Miller in Fort Smith.

Caldwell gave little encouragement to the school officials. In a report of his findings the attorney acknowledged that the U.S. Code and federal court decisions probably provided legal means to initiate an investigation of the Capital Citizens' Council's activities, but concluded that more evidence was necessary before ordering such an action. Caldwell stressed further that he had asked House whether the Little Rock school board would consider litigation of the sort carried out by Hoxie school officials, aimed at testing the 1957 interposition legislation. House had declined, but suggested that black attorneys might "be persuaded" to try such a suit.[29]

During the spring and summer segregationist propaganda targeted Faubus. Robert Ewing Brown published a statement contending that under a principle associated with state authority known as the police powers, the governor could order the "two races" to attend separate schools in order to "preserve tranquility." The principle, Brown claimed, also made Governor Faubus "immune to federal court orders."[30] In July the segregationist leader again wrote and published a letter calling on the governor to intervene in Little Rock to "avoid calamity."[31] Amis Guthridge kept up the pressure by publishing a newspaper advertisement which referred to the Texas governor's use of the Rangers to prevent desegregation after some disorder in Mansfield. The ad asked why Little Rock must have integration if the governor was able to prevent it in Texas.[32]

Segregationists also argued that passage of the state sovereignty commission bill represented a popular mandate that bound Faubus. East Arkansas pressed for action under the new law, but the bill could not become operative until the governor and lieutenant governor selected commissioners. The lieutenant governor, almost certainly following Faubus's direction, attempted to balance his appointments: his first choice was a legislator who had voted against the bill; his second was one of the measure's supporters from the Delta. This spurred an East Arkansas resident to seek a court order forcing the governor to fill the remaining seats.[33]

Amidst these developments the Little Rock NAACP was on the defensive. Passage of the anti-desegregation legislation and the appellate court decision in *Aaron* v. *Cooper* were setbacks.[34] Daisy Bates announced that the NAACP would challenge the 1957 laws in court, but at the end of July (perhaps due to Faubus's inaction in putting the commission into operation) there was still no suit.[35] After considerable speculation, Wiley Branton announced that the NAACP would not appeal the *Aaron* case to the U.S. Supreme Court. The branch decided as it did out of a concern, not made public, that the Supreme Court might follow the lower court, thereby establishing an unfortunate precedent.[36] Further complicating the NAACP's position in Little Rock were the activities of Dr. and Mrs. Lorch. Their commitment to the cause of racial justice was unswerving, but they were recognized as active Communists, which had led to legal action and adverse publicity and had resulted in a false but widespread impression that outsiders and subversives were influencing local NAACP affairs.[37]

Despite such difficulties, the NAACP expected desegregation to begin at Central on September 3 without resistance from the governor.[38] One member of the Arkansas NAACP wrote an analysis setting forth this view: Admittedly, Faubus would not defend integration; he would even promise to delay it legally if such were the "will of the people." But "the fact remains that he is not against integration and he is fairly certain that there is no legal means of preventing integration in the long run." Also, unlike any probable successor, the governor would "certainly do everything within his power to keep down violence

. . . [fully recognizing] the significance of violence and agitation to people in other states, as well as its reaction on people within the state." The victory over James Johnson, the observer concluded, indicated that Faubus would adhere to his position if it became necessary "to buck the extremists again."[39]

The governor's public statements and actions suggested some basis for this conclusion. Faubus refused official comment on the demands of Brown and Guthridge, although he did announce after the federal appellate decision in *Aaron* that desegregation in Little Rock was a "local problem," and that he saw no need to intervene.[40] Faubus's stand on the state sovereignty commission also suggested that he hoped in general to avoid any direct involvement with desegregation. Responding at a press conference to questions concerning segregationist claims that the commission and other measures made integration unnecessary, the governor stated, "Everyone knows that state laws can't supersede federal laws."[41] And he did not make commission appointments until compelled by court order; even then his selections included Shaver, a respected moderate.[42] Faubus further tried to distance himself from state attorney general Bennett's anti-desegregation position. There was wide speculation that Bennett was using the race issue to stir up support for a bid for the governor's office. During a congressional committee hearing for the 1957 Civil Rights Act, Bennett testified, receiving publicity as Arkansas's official representative. No doubt to counter this attention Faubus sent Shaver as his personal spokesman to outline for the committee the state's moderate but comparatively impressive progress in race relations.[43] On other occasions Governor Faubus pointed with pride to the desegregation of Arkansas universities and colleges and the near equalization of black and white teacher salaries. Faubus also refused to interfere with communities such as Hoxie and those in northwestern Arkansas that had already desegregated. In June the governor made one public pronouncement running counter to his previous actions in which he suggested that Little Rock, with its large black population, was perhaps not yet ready for desegregation.[44]

Privately, however, Faubus contacted the capital city's segregationist leaders. During July one of the governor's close as-

sociates, clothing store owner James T. Karam, arranged for
Faubus to meet with Guthridge, Brown, and an outspoken
minister identified with the segregationist cause, Rev. Wesley
Pruden. Accompanying Faubus was his legal advisor, William
J. Smith. Although the conversation was quite general, apparently some attention was given to delaying or preventing desegregation at Central, perhaps through the use of state police
troopers. The possibility of Faubus's running for a third gubernatorial term was also mentioned. Even though it seems unlikely that either Governor Faubus or Smith made any specific
commitments, the discussion gave segregationists the impression that some action might be possible that could prevent desegregation at Central. After the meeting, Guthridge occasionally was in touch with Faubus through Karam.[45]

CLIMAX: AUGUST 1957

By the end of July it was uncertain whether desegregation
would begin in Little Rock without incident. In the city itself,
community leaders had decided to change from a mayoral to a
city manager system of government. An election of commissioners would occur in November 1957, making Mayor W. W.
Mann a lame duck because his term of office would end in December; this undermined his influence and effectiveness. In addition, although it was clear that local police could be relied on
to do their duty, they had not been trained to handle possible
large-scale disorder.[46] On the state level, Faubus's support of
the segregationist legislation arising from his private trade-off
with East Arkansas on the tax increase created a legal and political dilemma. Although the constitutionality of the legislation
was doubtful, only the courts could ultimately decide one way
or the other, and litigation would take time. Until declared invalid, the laws represented a popular mandate which the governor could resist only at a high political cost—especially if he
hoped to run for a third term. At the same time, however, direct interference with Judge Miller's court order in *Aaron* would
raise an inevitable constitutional challenge.[47]

Complicating matters was the timidity of the federal government. President Eisenhower had provided little direct public

support for desegregation in general, and in a public statement in July 1957 he said that use of federal forces to enforce the principle was unlikely. Neither the president nor the Justice Department resisted Governor Allan Shivers's use of Rangers to reestablish segregation in several Texas communities after desegregation had resulted in disorderly crowds.[48] Division in the president's cabinet had also prevented vigorous executive lobbying for a new civil rights bill, which enabled southern congressional leaders to significantly weaken the measure during the summer of 1957.[49]

During August events moved toward a climax. A newspaper advertising campaign, regular meetings, and rallies heightened public awareness of the segregationists. Phone calls, letters, and telegrams to Governor Faubus demanded that he take a stand against desegregation of Central.[50] As tension mounted, attorney and school board member Wayne Upton decided to explore a new course of action. On August 13 he appeared before Judge Miller's court in Fort Smith as part of a pretrial hearing having nothing to do with desegregation. After the hearing he told Miller that he believed a suit would be filed in state court requesting a delay in the desegregation of Central until the constitutionality of the 1957 segregation legislation was determined. Miller replied that if such a case did develop, the school board should return to his court and he would consider ordering a stay until the constitutional question was settled.[51]

When Upton returned to Little Rock he and Blossom explored further the possibility of a suit. On the morning of August 15 the two talked with Faubus in very general terms about the meeting with Miller. That evening the school board members met with William J. Smith at Blossom's home. Blossom hoped that a court invalidation of the segregation laws would make it politically feasible for the governor to issue a public statement acknowledging Little Rock's constitutional duty to comply with Miller's order in *Aaron*. But the superintendent's hopes were dashed when neither Faubus nor Smith expressed a willingness to cooperate. The next day the issue became more complicated when Little Rock businessman William F. Rector filed in the local chancery court a suit requesting a judgment on the constitutionality of the 1957 measures. Apparently Upton was the only school board member who knew that Rector would file this case, but whether Upton was involved in initiating it is unclear.[52]

Following these developments school officials reconsidered their course of action. On Sunday, August 18, Blossom, Upton, and Harold J. Engstrom, another member of the school board, went to Fort Smith to meet again with Judge Miller. Discussing the newly filed suit, Miller suggested that another procedural approach (an injunction) might better serve the school board's purposes. The three returned to Little Rock and pondered the matter further. At some point Blossom may have even delivered to Faubus, for some undetermined reason, a petition like that filed by Rector. Finally, however, the board members decided against taking any legal measures and during the third week in August told the governor privately of their decision.[53] Several local black ministers began a suit in federal district court on August 20 that challenged the constitutionality of the segregation laws, but this was almost certainly an independent action not involving the school board.[54]

The situation soon acquired a still sharper focus. On August 22 Governor Marvin Griffin, a well-known segregationist from Georgia, spoke at a Capital Citizens' Council meeting in Little Rock, contending in vague but inflammatory terms that Georgia was using interposition to nullify the *Brown* decision. The idea that Georgia was able to circumvent the Supreme Court's mandate through legal means had a resounding impact on segregationists in the city. Although Griffin's contention was a distortion of the operation of interposition in Georgia, local segregationists used the claim to build up still more public pressure. The pressure became so great that Faubus increasingly came to question whether desegregation should begin on September 3. He had confused segregationists by letting Griffin stay in the governor's mansion while he had left town during the night of the CCC meeting. The next day the two governors had met over breakfast, but there had been discussion of neither the Georgia governor's speech nor integration in general.[55] But local segregationists did not know the impact of their campaign on Faubus.

Concerned over the growing intensity of segregationist pro-

test, Superintendent Blossom worked feverishly to avoid possible trouble, but with no success. On several occasions he privately urged the governor to make a public statement in support
of law and order; he also asked Judge Miller for such a statement. The judge declined. Faubus too refused, arguing that the
1957 segregation measures had given him a mandate supported by a large majority of Arkansas voters, and that failing
to enforce the "people's will" would have significant political
ramifications for himself and his neo-populist policies. The
governor said further that no public statement was possible until the courts decided on the legality of the 1957 legislation. Finally, Faubus told Blossom that Griffin's speech had generated
a major change of opinion in Little Rock. Prior to the speech
the city's citizens were resigned to the acceptance of desegregation; now they yearned to believe that Griffin was right about
interposition. This change could, the governor feared, lead to
violence and disorder if black children entered Central High on
schedule.[56]

As early as August 20 Faubus had called the Justice Department in Washington to discuss federal responsibility for preventing violence resulting from integration. Department authorities agreed to send A. B. Caldwell to talk privately with
Governor Faubus. On August 28 Faubus met with Caldwell and
asked what action the federal government intended to take to
prevent possible trouble in Little Rock. He expressed concern
about violence, but offered no evidence supporting such concern. The Justice Department attorney told the governor that
the federal government could do nothing until an incident occurred.[57]

Faced with a tense political environment, the school board's
refusal to test the segregation laws, and the timidity of the federal government, Faubus decided that a delay was essential. He
arranged privately to have a suit filed in Pulaski County chancery court on August 27 asking for a temporary injunction against
the school board. Mrs. Clyde A. Thomason, recording secretary of a recently formed segregationist organization known as
the Mothers' League of Central High School, was the plaintiff.
Expressing concern over possible trouble, she asked the court
to enjoin the school board from integrating Central.[58]

Other suits confused the legal scene. Earlier, Guthridge had filed a case for Mrs. Elva Wilburn and her daughter, seeking to force Little Rock school officials to allow white students at Central High to transfer to a segregated school on request. This case grew out of Guthridge's exchange with the school board in July; it apparently had no connection with the Faubus-initiated suit. On August 26 Attorney General Bennett also began litigation against the NAACP under legislation passed earlier in the year.[59]

Amidst the interplay of these public and private developments Faubus was headed for a confrontation. On August 29, 1957, both Faubus and Blossom gave testimony in the *Thomason* case. Faubus stated his fear that violence was likely if integration proceeded as planned; but he gave no explicit grounds for such fear. Blossom testified that he had no expectation of trouble, a statement not easily reconciled with his actions since the beginning of summer. On the basis of the governor's testimony the chancery court granted an injunction against implementation of the Blossom Plan.[60] Upon hearing of the local court's action, Judge Miller called the chief judge of the federal eighth circuit, asking to be relieved of further involvement with the Little Rock case. Taking Miller's place was federal district judge Ronald N. Davies, who had arrived in the city from North Dakota just three days before to handle a backlog of cases created by the retirement of Judge Trimble in 1956.[61] During the evening of the twenty-ninth Faubus met with his advisors; he repeated his concerns about disorder but again offered no specific justification for a course of action involving possible trouble. The next day the school board went before Judge Davies requesting an injunction against the chancery court's order, which the judge granted.[62]

Following the federal tribunal's decision Faubus met again with his advisors, though no further action resulted. There were more private meetings between Blossom and the governor, a meeting between Governor Faubus and the school board, and another between Faubus and Winthrop Rockefeller. On his own recognizance Faubus also placed the Arkansas National Guard on alert and asked William J. Smith to draw up a proclamation calling for the Guard's use at Central. By September 2 no one knew what to expect when the schools opened the following day.[63] The governor appeared on television on the evening of the second with an announcement that ended the uncertainty. He reviewed the state's progress toward desegregation over the preceding years, emphasizing his role as a moderate on race questions and a populist on social and economic issues. Faubus asserted that until Griffin's speech public opinion in the capital city accepted desegregation with resignation; after the Georgian spoke, however, the climate had changed and a majority of the city's population was now unsure as to the standing of the *Brown* decision in the Arkansas capital. Faubus noted, furthermore, that majorities in Little Rock and across the state had voted in favor of the interposition measures in November. As governor he was bound, he said, to enforce these laws until the "proper authority" determined their constitutionality.[64]

In his proclamation Faubus linked interposition to possible violence. He insisted that violence would occur if integration proceeded on schedule at Central the next day. His concern was based on reported increases in sales of various weapons, phone calls, rumors of segregationist caravans converging on Little Rock, and pleas from Superintendent Blossom. Governor Faubus referred to his testimony in the chancery court, and contended that, despite statements to the contrary, Blossom was also worried about possible disorder. Then he claimed that Judge Davies had foreclosed any possibility of testing the interposition measures. He blamed Blossom, the school board, and the federal courts for "forcing" integration on "the people" contrary to their will as demonstrated through "time-honored principles of Democracy" in the segregation measures of 1956 and 1957.[65] But underlying all this, as "one of the greatest reasons for unrest and for the imminence of disorder and violence," the governor exclaimed, was uncertainty over whether the interposition statutes or the Supreme Court's opinion constituted the law of the land. Faubus asserted that until this uncertainty was cleared up state law was supreme, and to preserve the peace, black children would not be permitted to enter Central High and whites would not be allowed in black schools. Units of the Arkansas National Guard were already stationed around the school to enforce this order; they were, the governor concluded, enforcing neither segregation nor integration, but preserving order.[66]

PUBLIC CONFRONTATION—SECRET NEGOTIATIONS

Overnight national and international attention focused on Little Rock as the school board wrestled with the consequences of Faubus's stand. After the governor's proclamation school officials asked the few black children scheduled to enter Central to stay home temporarily. Under the guidance of the NAACP and Daisy Bates, the children complied. On September 3 the board asked Judge Davies whether there could be a delay in integration until there was some resolution of the dilemma, but the school board's attorneys presented no evidence in support of this request. Without a showing of evidence, Davies ordered implementation of integration "forthwith." Davies based his order in part on a statement issued by Mayor Mann asserting that neither he nor the police had received any notice of impending trouble.[67]

On September 4 Faubus clashed directly with the federal district court, which, in turn, brought the intervention of the Justice Department. Following private orders from the governor, the National Guard blocked nine black children from entering Central. Elizabeth Eckford, one of the nine, attempted to enter the school alone, and in the process of being turned away received abusive racial epithets from a few members of a crowd near the school, though she was not physically hurt. Photographs of the incident appeared around the world, arousing understandable sympathy for the black young people's cause and casting a shadow over the public image of Arkansas.[68] Faced with these developments, Davies asked the Justice Department on September 5 to investigate the causes of the disruption of Little Rock's desegregation plan. In fact, the department had secretly begun such an investigation on its own; following Davies's request, however, the government's role became official.[69]

But other factors influenced the judge's resort to the Justice Department. On September 5, while formally asking Davies for a postponement in the implementation of the Blossom Plan, the school board privately urged the judge to call in United States marshals to carry out the desegregation order. Uncertainty arising from the board's conflicting positions and a desire to avoid direct confrontation between federal agents and state troops contributed to Davies's decision to call for an investigation to establish a factual basis for any legal action against Faubus.[70] Reinforcing this cautious approach was the outspoken recalcitrance of Arkansas's governor. With the public announcement of Davies's call for federal intervention Faubus telegrammed President Eisenhower, claiming that neither integration nor segregation was at issue in his confrontation with the federal court. Pointing to the successful record of desegregation in northwestern Arkansas, the governor asserted that the only real issue was whether the chief executive of a state could move to prevent violence and preserve law and order. He then charged that federal authorities had tapped his phone, were ready to arrest him, and were engaged in other pernicious activities.[71] Eisenhower denied these accusations and emphasized that the president would uphold the Constitution. Faubus responded by pointing out that Little Rock's aldermen had publicly supported his use of the Guard, and by making William J. Smith available to provide "certain evidence" justifying his position (though no such evidence was in fact forthcoming).[72]

The interplay of public and private developments perpetuated confrontation. On September 7 Judge Davies, again noting insufficient evidence, turned down the board's request for a suspension of his court order.[73] On the same day, in Washington, D.C., U.S. Attorney General Brownell and President Eisenhower met and discussed Little Rock. Eisenhower wanted to give Faubus every possible means for an "orderly retreat," as long as he ultimately complied with the court order; the president's administration would neither "compromise" nor "capitulate," however, if the governor continued to resist. On September 8 the Justice Department received word privately through an intermediary that Faubus sought to confer about some way to resolve the impasse, but after an exchange of views it became clear that no acceptable grounds for agreement existed. Both sides then ended negotiations.[74]

In Little Rock the duel between Governor Faubus and Judge Davies continued. By September 9 Davies received from U.S. Attorney Osro Cobb a detailed report of the FBI investigation initiated a week earlier. After thoroughly studying the report but not making its contents public, the judge directed the Justice Department to file a petition for an injunction against Governor Faubus. In his directions Davies stipulated that the governor should comply at once with the desegregation order, but he gave Faubus ten days to prepare for a full hearing of his position if he refused. On the same day Governor Faubus, arguing that the Supreme Court had made "deliberate speed" the standard for implementation of desegregation, criticized Judge Davies for demanding an immediate end to segregation. He asserted further that the judge ignored states' rights by substituting his judgment for the governor's as to potential disorder. Despite these verbal assaults, the governor followed his lawyer's advice and said that he would comply with final court orders. On the following day (the tenth) he accepted a summons for the trial set for September 20, but refused to withdraw the National Guard from Central.[75]

With more than a week to go before Faubus would have to present his case in federal court, private negotiations were resumed. Following the efforts of Arkansas congressman Brooks Hays, Faubus asked to confer with President Eisenhower, who agreed to a meeting in Newport, Rhode Island, on the fourteenth. But even though the governor acknowledged a duty to comply with court orders, nothing concrete resulted from the conference except heightened tension and another round of private exchanges with the Justice Department, with Hays serving as intermediary.[76] By the eighteenth the Justice Department acknowledged that it would not press for an injunction in the September 20 trial if Faubus would remove the Guard and allow desegregation to proceed at Central. Negotiations came to focus on finding some means for Faubus to retreat without making it seem that he was backing down willingly. Hays suggested that Eisenhower federalize the National Guard, thus displacing the governor's authority. Presidential advisor Sherman Adams did not favor the idea, however, and with this option closed off Faubus terminated negotiations.[77]

Following the defeat of Hays's efforts, public attention turned to Judge Davies's court in Little Rock. On September 19 attorneys for the governor filed a lengthy affidavit contesting Davies's jurisdiction, but at trial on the twentieth the judge rejected these contentions. Apparently expecting such a result, the lawyers gave notice that they would no longer participate and walked out. Davies continued the hearing, however, and the Justice Department presented testimony from 8 of the 105 witnesses it had subpoenaed, which addressed the question of whether a potential for violence or disorder existed during the time when Central was scheduled to begin desegregation on September 3. The testimony uniformly agreed that no grounds for concern about violence existed prior to and including the third of September. No other issues were explored. The Justice Department made no effort to introduce as evidence the FBI report, which contained the facts that had originally convinced Davies that judicial proceedings against Faubus were necessary. On the basis of the federal government's case Davies granted an injunction against the governor, who within hours complied by withdrawing the Guard and then left Arkansas for a conference in Georgia. Before leaving Faubus exclaimed that his "crucifixion" would begin shortly; perhaps to forestall such an eventuality, his attorneys prepared an appeal.[78]

In Little Rock, tension filled the air during the weekend before the opening of Central to the nine black children on September 23.[79] School officials again asked Davies for federal marshals to back up city police, but the judge sent them to U.S. Attorney Cobb instead. Cobb explained that he needed "specific authority from the Department of Justice to seek an order from the federal judge for United States marshals' . . . help in protecting the Negro students." Cobb called Washington but "did not get the authority from the department."[80] Perhaps the Justice Department turned down the request for federal marshals because its one liaison with the Little Rock police informed them that state troopers would come to the aid of the city authorities on request. When school officials learned of the availability of state police they decided to go ahead with their desegregation plan.[81]

On September 23 and 24 Little Rock's bad times became even

worse. The black young people entered Central on Monday, but disturbances inside and outside the school resulted in their withdrawal after a few hours.[82] Once U.S. Attorney Brownell was notified about the trouble he called President Eisenhower, who gave permission to use federal authority to prevent further obstruction of federal court orders. The next day, as a crowd again gathered at Central, Mayor Mann, who had maintained phone communication with White House aide Maxwell Rabb, formally requested federal intervention. Rabb had approved the wording of the mayor's statement beforehand and plans to use federal troops if the need arose had been worked out in advance. Immediately following the mayor's request, Eisenhower federalized the Arkansas National Guard and ordered the secretary of defense to deal with resistance through whatever means were necessary, including the use of regular U.S. military personnel. The president's decision was carried out through an executive order that had been drafted by the Justice Department and had as its legal basis provisions of the U.S. Code.[83]

Eisenhower's action created a superficial calm in Little Rock, but beneath the calm lay tension, resentment, and uncertainty. Units of the elite 101st Airborne quickly established order around Central High, but the appearance of regular U.S. Army troops stunned the community. Moderates, already demoralized and divided over what they considered distorted media reporting of the events after September 3, became totally fragmented after the twenty-fourth. With the streets quiet, attention turned to the plight of the few black children attending integrated classes at Central. Despite the best efforts of the school administration and the school board, and the clear neutrality of most white students toward them, the children suffered relentless harassment from a small but well-organized group of segregationist-supported youths within the school.[84] All of this built up more support for Governor Faubus in the capital and across the state and encouraged him to take an increasingly segregationist stance toward desegregation, states' rights, and the federal judiciary.

And inevitably the fall crisis generated litigation. The segregationist Mothers' League pushed cases in federal court challenging the Phase Program and the constitutionality of President Eisenhower's use of federal troops, and another suit tested the president's action in state court. The NAACP initiated or continued suits testing the constitutionality of the state sovereignty commission and contested several laws being used by Arkansas Attorney General Bennett to open the organization's records to public scrutiny. Also under way was Faubus's appeal of Davies's judgment against him, which raised issues involving the constitutionality of the governor's interference with federal court orders from September 3 to 20.[85]

By the end of 1957 states' rights defiance, racial antagonism, and public disorder had shattered Faubus's moderate, populist image. Superficially, the explanation for the change seemed clear: the governor had taken the stand at Central to insure his election to a third gubernatorial term. But the political trade involving the tax increase, the secret meetings with segregationists, school board members, and a representative of the Justice Department, and sponsorship of the *Thomason* suit did not necessarily represent the calculated maneuvering of a demagogue. Instead, these developments may be understood in terms of Faubus's attempt to accommodate the "popular mandate" represented by the interposition laws, segregationists' assertions regarding police powers, and public confusion over what in fact constituted the law of the land. By searching for a politically expedient accommodation, the governor sought above all to force the federal government to accept responsibility for enforcement of its own court order. Even amidst inflammatory attacks on Judge Davies after September 3, Faubus held steadfastly to his overriding purpose by acknowledging an unqualified duty to obey "final" court orders. The same determination underlay the secret negotiations with the Justice Department. Only after the federal government failed to introduce the FBI report into evidence during the September 20 trial and the short-sighted decision to use combat paratroopers rather than federalized national guardsmen or U.S. marshals on the twenty-fourth did Faubus embrace an outright segregationist stance.

NOTES

1. *SSN*, Dec. 1956, 8.
2. FBI Report—Little Rock, 44–12284–933, text of Governor Fau-

bus's proclamation, Sept. 2, 1957, ordering Arkansas National Guard units to Central High.

3. Virgil T. Blossom to Leon B. Catlett and A. F. House, Nov. 8, 1956, LBCF.

4. House to Blossom, Nov. 13, 1956, LBCF.

5. *SSN*, Jan. 1956, 8.

6. Ibid., Mar. 1957, 13.

7. Ibid.

8. Ibid. Orval Eugene Faubus, *Down from the Hills* (Little Rock, 1980), 167.

9. *SSN*, Mar. 1957, 13.

10. "An Analysis of the Provisions of the Johnson Amendment," DBP (SHSW, AD), MS. 523, Box 5, Folder 8.

11. *SSN*, Mar. 1957, 13. Daisy Bates, *The Long Shadow of Little Rock, A Memoir* (New York, 1962), 53–56.

12. *SSN*, Mar. 1957, 13. Faubus, *Down from the Hills*, 174.

13. Faubus, *Down from the Hills*, 148, 151, 157, 159, 161, 164–69, 173.

14. Ibid., 157. Orval E. Faubus, interview with author, July 15, 1980. William J. Smith, interview with author, Sept. 3, 1980.

15. *SSN*, Feb. 1957, 3.

16. Faubus, *Down from the Hills*, 169. I first learned of the connection between interposition and the tax program in an interview with Marcus Halbrook of the Arkansas Legislative Council; Faubus interview, July 15, 1980, confirmed the connection. See also Faubus, *Down from the Hills*, 148, 151, 157, 159, 161, 164–169, 173.

17. Faubus, *Down from the Hills*, 166, 173, 175.

18. *SSN*, Mar. 1957, 14; Apr. 1957, 15.

19. See chap. 1 for discussion of this voting pattern. See also "Little Rock, Arkansas, School Desegregation Fall 1959," Dwight D. Eisenhower Library Staff Files, James C. Hagerty Papers, 1953–1961, Integration—Little Rock, Box 6, 6.

20. *SSN*, Apr. 1957, 15.

21. Ibid. Robert L. Carter to Leon B. Catlett, Jan. 21, 1957, LBCF; Bates, *Long Shadow*, 52–53. *Aaron* v. *Cooper*, 2 *RRLR* 593 (U.S.C.A. 8th Cir. 1957). See also *SSN*, May 1957, 2; June 1957, 9.

22. House to Catlett, Feb. 15, 1957.

23. *SSN*, July 1957, 10. See chap. 3 for discussion of the *Hoxie* case.

24. *SSN*, Aug. 1957, 7.

25. Ibid. See also "Little Rock . . . Desegregation," James C. Hagerty Papers.

26. *SSN*, Aug. 1957, 7; "Little Rock . . . Desegregation," James C. Hagerty Papers. See also chap. 1 for discussion of the "class flaw" in the Blossom Plan.

27. *SSN*, Aug. 1957, 7. See also a draft of the statement in LBCF;

and Virgil T. Blossom, *It Has Happened Here* (New York, 1959), 43.

28. See Blossom interview, FBI Report 44–12284–933, pp. 85–100; Numan V. Bartley, "Looking Back at Little Rock," *Arkansas Historical Quarterly*, 25 (Summer 1966), 105–111; Blossom, *It Has Happened Here*, 40–75. See also Faubus, *Down from the Hills*, 174.

29. Arthur B. Caldwell to Warren Olney III, July 24, 1957, "Segregation in Public Schools in Arkansas," #144–100–9, A. B. Caldwell Papers, Special Collections, University Library, University of Arkansas, Fayetteville (hereafter cited as ABCP [UAF]). I am grateful to Dr. Michal R. Belknap for this reference.

30. *SSN*, June 1957, 9. See also Amis Guthridge interview, DDEP (1972).

31. *SSN*, July 1957, 10.

32. Guthridge interview, DDEP (1972), pp. 1–30. Faubus, *Down from the Hills*, 187–88. See also Bartley, "Looking Back," 105–111; Blossom, *It Has Happened Here*, 40–75; Bates, *Long Shadow*, 53.

33. *SSN*, Apr. 1957, 15; July 1957, 10; Aug. 1957, 9. Emmett E. Miller interview on L. R. Lukes tape, FBI Report 44–12285–855. Faubus, *Down from the Hills*, 161, 165–66, 167–169, 173.

34. Bates, *Long Shadow*, 53–56.

35. *SSN*, Apr. 1957, 15; Aug. 1957, 7.

36. Ibid., Aug. 1957, 7. Wiley Branton interview, DDEP (1973); Wiley Branton, interview with author, Dec. 11, 1979.

37. *SSN*, May 1957, 2. See chap. 5 for further discussion.

38. Branton interview, Dec. 11, 1979.

39. Anonymous memorandum, NAACP Group III, Series B. General Office File 199, Folder 1, 1957, School, Arkansas, General Correspondence (Library of Congress).

40. *SSN*, June 1957, 9.

41. Ibid., Aug. 1957, 7.

42. Ibid., Sept. 1957, 7.

43. Ibid., Apr. 1957, 15. *Civil Rights Hearings before Subcommittee No. 5 of the Committee on the Judiciary, House of Representatives, Eighty-Fifth Congress, First Session* (Washington, D.C., 1957), 1183.

44. Faubus, *Down from the Hills*, 174; *SSN*, July 1957, 10.

45. Guthridge interview, DDEP (1972), 12–14.

46. Bartley, "Looking Back," 105–106.

47. Ibid., 111–116. Faubus, *Down from the Hills*, 180.

48. J. W. Peltason, *Fifty-Eight Lonely Men: Southern Federal Judges and School Desegregation* (New York, 1961), 144–46. John Thomas Elliff, "The United States Department of Justice and Individual Rights, 1937–1962" (Ph.D. diss., Harvard University, 1967), 420–462.

49. Elliff, "Department of Justice," 429–433.

50. Bates, *Long Shadow*, 57–58. Blossom, *It Has Happened Here*, 30–

49. Faubus, *Down from the Hills*, 187–188, 192, 200–201. FBI Report 44–12284–933, 19–21, 78, 83.

51. FBI Report 44–12284–933, interviews with Blossom, Upton, William J. Smith, Harold J. Engstrom, 76–77, 83, 94–95, 103–104, 112–116. The substance of the FBI interviews presented here and in the following paragraphs was confirmed by my own interviews with Mr. Smith, Mr. Upton, Mr. Engstrom, and Mr. Faubus.

52. Ibid. For facts on the Rector suit see William F. Rector interview, FBI Report 44–12284–937, 17–18. The jurisdictional basis of Rector's suit was an Arkansas statute of 1953 giving taxpayers in the Little Rock school district with children in the public schools standing to challenge decisions of the school board. See also "Complaint for Declaratory Judgment," 13, in FBI Report 44–12284–937. See also *SSN*, Sept. 1957, 6.

53. See note 50 above; and Faubus, *Down from the Hills*, 201. At Mr. Engstrom's behest, Blossom informed Judge Miller of the decision not to pursue a court test of the 1957 legislation; Harold J. Engstrom interview, FBI Report 44–12284–937, 236–238. For board members informing Faubus of their decision, see memo, Arthur B. Caldwell to Warren Olney III, Aug. 30, 1957, "Conference with Governor of Arkansas, August 28, 1957," #144–100–9, ABCP (UAF).

54. *SSN*, Sept. 1957, 6. *Smith* v. *Faubus*, 2 *RRLR* 1103 (U.S.C.A. 8th Cir. 1957). See also Bates, *Long Shadow*, 53–56.

55. *SSN*, Sept. 1957, 6. "Memorandum from A. B. Caldwell to Assistant Attorney General Warren Olney III," in FBI Report 44–12284–933, 23–24. Caldwell, an attorney for the Justice Department, was an Arkansan whom Faubus talked with in a private conference on Aug. 28, 1957. During the conference one of the concerns Faubus expressed was that the mood of Little Rock had changed from reluctant acceptance of integration to opposition because of Griffin's speech. This view is reiterated in Faubus, *Down from the Hills*, 195; and shared by Blossom, *It Has Happened Here*, 54; and Hays, *A Southern Moderate Speaks* (Chapel Hill, 1959), 153. See also Bartley, "Looking Back," 109.

56. The connections between Griffin's speech and interposition and Faubus's political situation are noted in Hays, *Southern Moderate*, 187; and Blossom, *It Has Happened Here*, 53–54. The importance of these related themes is developed further in "Memorandum from Caldwell to Olney," 23–25, and Blossom interview, 83, 97–98, 104, in FBI Report 44–12284–933. See also Faubus, *Down from the Hills*, 187. In an interview with the author on July 15, 1980, Faubus noted his responsibility for enforcing the interposition measures until they were declared invalid by the courts; he noted, too, that this obligation placed him in a difficult political situation as Sept. 3 neared.

57. See "Memorandum from Caldwell to Olney," FBI Report 44–12284–933; and Faubus, *Down from the Hills*, 197–198. In his treatment of the meeting with Caldwell, Faubus does not state that he told the Justice Department attorney that he had arranged the chancery court suit; he does admit, however, that it was through his efforts that the suit was filed; see Faubus, *Down from the Hills*, 201. This conclusion is supported further by Faubus's statement at a meeting with the school board; Blossom interview, 96, FBI Report 44–12284–933. See also Elliff, "Department of Justice," 463–466.

58. Faubus, *Down from the Hills*, 197–198, 201; "Memorandum from Caldwell to Olney," FBI Report 44–12284–933. See also Elliff, "Department of Justice," 429–433.

59. *SSN*, Sept. 1957, 6. On the Wilburn suit, see also House to Attorney Group, Aug. 25, 1957, LBCF.

60. The chancery hearing and the federal court proceedings are discussed in "Memorandum from Caldwell to Olney," 24–26, and Blossom interview, 96, in FBI Report 44–12284–933; Blossom, *It Has Happened Here*, 60–62; Bates, *Long Shadow*, 57; Faubus, *Down from the Hills*, 199, 201–203; *SSN*, Sept. 1957, 6.

61. Elliff, "Department of Justice," 464–465; and Ronald N. Davies interview with author, Apr. 16, 1980.

62. Elliff, "Department of Justice," 464–465; Davies interview, Apr. 16, 1980; Faubus, *Down from the Hills*, 199–204, 206–207. The meetings with Faubus's advisors are discussed in interviews with each advisor present, FBI Report 44–12284–933, 43–73. For the private meetings between Faubus and Blossom following the federal court's decision see Blossom interview, 97–98, 100, FBI Report 44–12284–933; and Blossom, *It Has Happened Here*, 66.

63. FBI Report 44–12284–933, 43–73. Faubus, *Down from the Hills*, 199–204, 206–207.

64. See full text of Governor Faubus's announcement on Sept. 2, 1957, in FBI Report 44–12284–933, 30–40.

65. Ibid. Faubus never gave convincing proof supporting his claim that violence would occur. In *Down from the Hills*, 198–204, 206, Faubus contends that Blossom was his primary source for this perception. The bulk of FBI Report 44–12284–933 is devoted to tracing down rumors concerning possible violence and to determining the validity of Faubus's claims. After an extensive investigation the FBI report concluded that, other than a few rumors, there was no basis for Faubus's claim that violence was likely when Central opened on Sept. 3. The FBI Report also shows that even the rumors grew out of a few minor incidents that had no connection with integration.

66. Faubus, *Down from the Hills*, 199–204, 206–207; FBI Report 44–12284–933, 30–40.

67. *SSN*, Oct. 1957, 1–3. Bates, *Long Shadow*, 63. Blossom, *It Has Happened Here*, 75.

68. Bates, *Long Shadow*, 69–71. Blossom, *It Has Happened Here*, 80. Faubus, *Down from the Hills*, 206–208, 210–212.

69. Elliff, "Department of Justice," 466–467, 469; Osro Cobb, "*United States* v. *Governor Orval E. Faubus et Al.*" (manuscript, University of Arkansas at Little Rock, Archives, n.d.). See also *SSN*, Oct. 1957, 2–5.

70. Elliff, "Department of Justice," 469; *SSN*, Oct. 1957, 2–5.

71. *SSN*, Oct. 1957, 1–3. Cobb, "*U.S.* v. *Faubus*." Faubus, *Down from the Hills*, 244.

72. *SSN*, Oct. 1957, 1–3. Blossom, *It Has Happened Here*, 89.

73. *SSN*, Oct. 1957, 1–3. Blossom, *It Has Happened Here*, 89.

74. Elliff, "Department of Justice," 470–471.

75. *SSN*, Oct. 1957, 1–3. Cobb, "*U.S.* v. *Faubus*."

76. *SSN*, Oct. 1957, 1–3. Cobb, "*U.S.* v. *Faubus*." W. J. Smith, interview with author, Sept. 3, 1980. Hays, *Southern Moderate*, 145–151. Faubus, *Down from the Hills*, 241, 255–258. Elliff, "Department of Justice," 472–473.

77. Elliff, "Department of Justice," 474–475.

78. *SSN*, Oct. 1957, 1–3. Cobb, "*U.S.* v. *Faubus*." Bates, *Long Shadow*, 83. Wiley Branton, interview with author, Dec. 11, 1979. Blossom, *It Has Happened Here*, 94–97. Elliff, "Department of Justice," 476–477. Faubus, *Down from the Hills*, 259–266. *Faubus* v. *U.S.*, 3 *RRLR* 439 (U.S.C.A. 8th Cir. 1958).

79. See note 78 above.

80. Elliff, "Department of Justice," 477.

81. Ibid., 478.

82. Ibid., 474–475.

83. Ibid., 478–479. See chap. 5 for further discussion.

84. Elizabeth Huckaby, *Crisis at Central High, Little Rock, 1957–58* (Baton Rouge, 1980) and Blossom, *It Has Happened Here*, 98–176, describe events within Central from the school administration's point of view. For the perspective of the black children and the NAACP, see DBP (SHSW, AD), and Bates, *Long Shadow*, 63–116. Aside from these sources, for the level of harassment see the briefs filed for *Aaron* v. *Cooper, Petition for Writ of Certiorari to the United States Court of Appeals for the Eighth Circuit, in the Supreme Court of the United States, October Term, 1958*. The issues raised in these and other sources will be considered in chap. 6.

85. These cases are cited and analyzed in chap. 6.

A Constitutional
Crisis _____ 5

Beneath the headlines reporting the confrontation in Little Rock lay a more complex story, touched upon but not analyzed in depth by the media, concerning the interplay of constitutional principles, political exigencies, and legal technicalities that shaped the actions of the governor, the federal government, the school board, and the NAACP. Central to the process of interaction were private negotiations and procedural maneuverings which gave direction to public events. Developments outside the public purview during the fateful summer and fall of 1957 fused constitutional issues with political considerations. Consideration of these developments helps explain why Judge Davies's decision against Governor Faubus and President Eisenhower's resort to military force neither brought unchallenged compliance with *Brown* nor ended confrontation.

FAUBUS SUBVERTS THE CONSTITUTION

Governor Faubus justified his defiance of Judge Miller's 1956 court order on the grounds that disorder was "imminent" and that only the intervention of military force could prevent it. But reference to increased sales of various weapons, communications with Superintendent Blossom, and rumors of car caravans descending on Little Rock obscured the legal basis underlying the governor's resort to force. At the center of this legal justification was a principle known as police powers—a broad but vaguely defined authority, inherent in the office of chief executive, to control persons and property in the interest of the general security, health, safety, morals, and welfare of the community.[1]

Though the police powers are extensive, they are subject to legal and constitutional limitations, as defined by the courts. Faubus's use of the Arkansas National Guard to exclude black children from Central High School raised the issue of whether he acted within limits accepted by the judiciary as constitutional. In part this issue turned on the reality of the threat of violence, but there was also a more fundamental problem: in the face of threatened disorder, it was the governor's duty to use his authority to preserve constitutional rights, not to deny them.[2]

Faubus's action was contrary even to states' rights doctrines. A fundamental assumption of states' rights was that governmental conduct was ultimately accountable to a majority of citizens in the local community. A policy initiated by a community's democratically elected representatives embodied the highest expression of sovereign authority, and any lawful exercise of police power must be in accord with this authority. More concretely, the voluntary plan of integration embodied in Little Rock's Phase Program represented the will of the local community as expressed by the majority's elected representatives, the city's school board. The March 1957 school board elections, giving Wayne Upton and Henry Rath nearly two-to-one victories over segregationist candidates, in effect reaffirmed the majority's support for their representatives' policy. According to states' rights logic, then, a lawful use of police powers would require a governor to assist local officials in the implementation of their program.[3]

States' rights doctrines, of course, had only minimal standing in American constitutional jurisprudence. But twentieth-century judicial precedents sustain the same result as that compelled by these doctrines. In 1909 the United States Supreme Court had upheld wide discretionary authority in a governor's handling of civil strife. "When it comes to a decision by the head of the state upon a matter involving its life, the ordinary rights of individuals must yield to what he deems the necessities of the moment," the Court said.[4] This principle was strikingly close to that proclaimed by segregationist leader Brown. Amidst the dislocations of the Great Depression, however, federal judges had significantly narrowed the range of the 1909 precedent. Although the state executive's authority was broad, the Court held in 1932, it did not follow that "every sort of action the Governor may take, no matter how justified . . . or subversive of private right . . . is conclusively supported by mere executive fiat."[5]

What constituted "allowable limits" of discretion was left to the courts, and these limits did not include "subversion" of constitutional rights established by federal authority. A governor could use military force to deal with potential or actual disorder, the Court said. But the "proper use" of such force was to maintain the federal court's jurisdiction, "not to attempt to override it; to aid in making its process effective and not to nullify it; to remove, and not to create, obstructions to the exercise . . . of . . . rights as judicially declared." A governor facing disorder that threatened citizens' "lawful rights" violated his duty if he used his "forces to assist in carrying out the unlawful purposes of those who created the disorders, or by suppressing rights which it is the duty of the state to defend."[6]

To use police or troops to suppress constitutional rights in the name of law and order, as a lower federal court put it, would be to "breed violence." Those seeking to destroy the citizens' rights would see that the government would assist them "if they gathered in sufficient numbers to constitute a menace to life." Thus any rule permitting a governor or other public official charged with enforcement of the law "to disregard the very law which it was his duty to enforce, in order to pacify a mob or suppress an insurrection, would deprive all citizens of any security in the enjoyment of their lives, liberty, or property."[7]

Clearly, then, segregationists' claims that Governor Faubus could lawfully act outside the jurisdiction of the federal court to maintain segregation were unfounded. Similarly, Faubus's assertion that a duty to maintain community peace and order overrode an obligation to defend constitutional rights established by the federal courts misconstrued the police powers principle. Thus, the governor should have used the Guard to *carry out* rather than *prevent* integration. However unfair (or even wrong) he may have considered such action, the proper course for Faubus to have pursued, if indeed he considered disorder "imminent" prior to the opening of Central on September 3, was to use his authority in support of the federal court order.[8]

This was the finding of Judge Davies after the September 20 trial,[9] and he was sustained by the U.S. Circuit Court of Appeals. To uphold the governor's position, the appellate court said, would mean that the "fiat of a state Governor and not the Constitution of the United States . . . [was] the supreme law of the land . . . [and] restrictions of the Federal Constitution upon the exercise of state power would be but impotent phrases." Under the American system of government such a view was "obviously untenable. There is no such avenue of escape from the paramount authority of the Federal Constitution."[10]

Faubus, of course, complied with Davies's order of September 20; but if he was willing eventually to accept the authority of the federal court, why had he initiated a confrontation in the first place? The governor's concern about potential harm to life and property seems at best only a partial answer to this question,[11] for he could as easily have used his police powers in defense of the constitutional rights of the black children and the authority of the federal judiciary. Rejection of this avenue of action strongly suggests that other factors were involved.

No doubt political considerations contributed to the governor's decision to use the Guard, but it is by no means certain that these involved only a narrow preoccupation with running for a third gubernatorial term.[12] What is certain is that Faubus had the rest of his administration to carry out the neo-populist program that he had worked diligently and skillfully to create. It was likely that during this period integration would continue to confuse and distort the politics of implementing the program. Thus Arkansas's economic and social improvement and the governor's administrative effectiveness seemed bound up with the integration issue. As Guthridge, Brown, and other segregationist spokesmen hammered home their interposition arguments, Faubus found himself in a position demanding a resolute stand. The governor could avoid the political implications of the interposition mandate established in the 1956 general election and in the assembly session of 1957 only by a policy of delay or by shifting to someone else the responsibility for enforcement of integration in Little Rock.[13]

Delay and shifting the burden were consistent with the accommodationist policy the governor had pursued since the Johnson challenge in 1956.[14] This policy led to the private sponsorship of the *Thomason* suit on August 19, 1957. Prior to that date Faubus, the segregationists, and the school board were unsure what the others would do, though contacts among them suggested possibilities.[15] In part the *Thomason* case resulted from the governor's struggle to find some way out of the uncertainties of the immediate situation, but in a larger sense it was the culmination of the summer's behind-the-scenes maneuvers. For Governor Faubus one primary goal of such maneuvering was the accommodation of segregationist interests without threatening his own integrity or that of his programs. But the incompatibility of Faubus's testimony with that given by Blossom raised a question of credibility, which in turn heightened tension. This, combined with Judge Davies's replacement of Miller, injected more confusion into Little Rock's integration experience. Not until after these occurrences did Faubus place the Guard on alert.[16]

With the proclamation of September 2 the governor set off a constitutional confrontation. As the confrontation persisted, Faubus repeated that he would adhere to a final decision by the courts as to the validity of his stand. He carried on private negotiations with the Justice Department on September 8–9, and concurred in Congressman Brooks Hays's efforts to end the crisis by presidential federalization of the National Guard.[17] He acquiesced in the latter two points, no doubt, because the president's action would—like a court decision—make federal authorities responsible for enforcement of integration. This would remove from Faubus the political stigma of involvement in the implementation of the Blossom Plan.

THE JUSTICE DEPARTMENT VACILLATES

The decision to confront federal authority in Little Rock was Governor Faubus's alone, but it grew out of complex developments, central among them being the role of the federal government, particularly the Justice Department. While Faubus pursued a legal strategy that inevitably generated conflict, the Justice Department made policy choices that contributed to such an outcome. Enmeshed in these choices were political and constitutional issues not unlike those involved in the governor's exercise of police powers.

The Justice Department's involvement with integration in Little Rock dated at least from early summer of 1957. In June, A. F. House had gone to Washington to discuss the impact of segregationist activity on the city. As a result, Justice Department attorney A. B. Caldwell went to Arkansas and reported that an FBI investigation of Capital Citizens' Council activities might reveal "conspiracies on the part of private individuals to interfere" with the school board in its efforts to comply with *Brown.* In the *Hoxie* case the U.S. Circuit Court of Appeals had construed the U.S. Code to mean that such "conspiracies" were unlawful. The court's decision meant, too, that the federal government possessed authority to intervene in such cases, though the limits of that authority were unclear.[18]

Yet Caldwell advised against premature intervention. He wrote that he had informed House of the possibility that the school board could obtain an injunction against the segregationists, like that obtained in the *Hoxie* case; and to the Justice Department he suggested that unless the Little Rock school board acted on its own, "we would be wiser to wait until receipt of more evidence of affirmative action" by the CCC before commencing any investigation. The attorney urged, however, that the Little Rock office of the FBI follow local events closely. The city's office should "promptly" inform the Justice Department of "any and all activities of the Capital Citizens Council . . . in connection with the integration of Little Rock schools."[19]

The Justice Department kept all this from the governor. He privately made contact with Washington on August 20; on the twenty-eighth he had a lengthy discussion with Caldwell about integration in Little Rock. From these exchanges Faubus learned only that federal decisions to intervene depended primarily on a request from local authorities, as in Hoxie, or on the order of a federal judge, as in Clinton, Tennessee. Yet it was possible that the federal government might simply remain silent, as it

had done after Governor Shivers's actions in Texas. At no time
did the Justice Department inform the governor that the U.S.
Code sanctioned federal involvement of the sort outlined in
Caldwell's June report.[20]

The Justice Department remained cautious even after September 3. When word of Faubus's proclamation reached Washington, Attorney General Herbert Brownell ordered department lawyers to "study the constitutional questions of the right
of the federal court to review the governor's discretion and to
enjoin him if it should be found that his action was without
justification."[21] While this study was pending, the department
considered three possible courses of action: to initiate contempt
proceedings against Faubus and the National Guard com-
mander for violation of a court order, to advise the president to
federalize the National Guard and order it to enforce integration, or to obtain from the federal court a decision as to the legality of the governor's obstructionism. Brownell decided to
pursue the third course—but only upon a direct request from
the federal court.[22]

The result was delay. On September 3, responding to an initiative by the school board, Judge Davies ordered integration to
proceed "forthwith." Yet the Guard stayed on duty around
Central High and the federal government took no official action. The following day the black children attempted to enter
the school and the Guard prevented them. At this point school
officials could have requested federal intervention; instead, they
asked Davies for a temporary postponement of integration. The
school board also privately requested the help of federal marshals. Aware that such action would set off an immediate clash,
Davies formally requested an investigation by the Justice Department. Promptly complying with the request, the federal
government finally became an official party to the Little Rock
controversy.[23]

The Justice Department's findings went against Faubus on
almost every point. For one thing, department attorneys established solid constitutional grounds for reviewing and prohibit-
ing Faubus's obstruction of court orders. About the same time,
an FBI inquiry turned up "documentary proof" that the governor had explicitly ordered the troops to keep black children

out of Central. The FBI's report also stated that Faubus's claims about excessive sales of weapons were groundless or at most based on vague rumor, and that no local officials had sought the governor's intervention (though it did document Blossom's numerous statements concerning possible trouble).[24] On the basis of this evidence the department charged that Governor Faubus had initiated "a deliberate nullification of the Constitution and laws of the United States," as well as "a frustration of the orders of the district court."[25]

Despite this vigorous language no direct action was taken against Faubus. To recapitulate, on September 7 Davies turned down the school board's request for a postponement. In Washington President Eisenhower told Brownell of his desire to give the governor "every opportunity to make an orderly retreat," as long as he complied with the federal court's rulings.[26] On September 8 and 9 occurred the private (and ultimately unsuccessful) negotiations between department representatives and the governor's intermediary. Once these talks broke down, U.S. Attorney Cobb turned over the FBI report to Judge Davies. After studying the detailed evidence, the judge ordered the Justice Department to seek a preliminary injunction against Governor Faubus.[27] Davies could have asked the department to request a temporary restraining order or to initiate contempt proceedings, either of which would have required Faubus to comply immediately or face criminal prosecution.[28]

Davies's choice of a preliminary injunction was significant: it gave Faubus time to prepare a case defending his actions. Davies made this choice because he "was reluctant to believe that a governor of a State would deliberately and intentionally use his troops to obstruct the orders of a Federal Court." The judge was also "definitely of the view that the Governor should be served with notice and afforded an opportunity to be heard before any injunction issued against him or his officers."[29] U.S. Attorney Cobb initiated the pleading process on September 10; Davies set the hearing for the twentieth.

During the ten days before the hearing, the Justice Department privately developed plans that in the long run would have a great impact on Little Rock. Attorney General Brownell, expecting that the Arkansas governor would continue to resist federal authority even if he lost in court on September 20, ordered Justice Department lawyers to study every conceivable maneuver left to the governor. They found that Faubus might comply with a court order, defy it by continuing to exclude black children, or close Central High by executive order. Regardless of which of these courses he followed, continued involvement by the federal government seemed likely.[30] More significantly, department officials recommended that intervention by U.S. military personnel, at the order of President Eisenhower himself, would best meet all contingencies.

To justify such a course, department lawyers prepared memoranda attempting to establish a legal and constitutional basis for the president's use of regular military troops and federalized national guardsmen in a state where there was defiance of federal law and authority.[31] In doing so, they were careful to avoid Section 331 of the U.S. Code, under which a request of the state legislature or governor was made prerequisite to use of military force by the president.[32] Instead, they relied on two other sections of the Code, 332 and 333, which authorized presidential discretion. These provisions gave the president the power to send troops into a state to remove obstructions "against the authority of the United States," or put down violence which hindered the execution of the "law of the United States." They not only displaced Section 331; they also superseded another federal statute which prohibited the president from employing the U.S. Army as a "posse comitatus . . . for the purpose of executing the laws." This statute allowed an exception where "employment of said force may be expressly authorized by the Constitution or by act of Congress"; Section 332 qualified for that exception, Justice insisted, for it authorized the president to "use such of the armed forces as he considers necessary to enforce . . . laws or to suppress . . . rebellion."[33]

As these legal intricacies were being worked out, tensions mounted amidst repeated failures to negotiate a compromise. The preparations for and the inconclusive results of Eisenhower's conference with Faubus at Newport on September 14 attracted extensive media coverage. On the eighteenth and nineteenth, through Congressman Hays, Faubus and the Justice Department again entered into private negotiations. Hays knew that the federal government was reluctant to face a "show-down of force against force," and suggested that the federalization of the National Guard would avoid such a showdown while giving Faubus a politically safe justification for withdrawal. These negotiations ended after Sherman Adams resisted Hays's idea. But in large measure the possibility was already foreclosed by the Justice Department's distrust of the governor as indicated by its preparations to use the army. Moreover, the department was committed to a full-scale hearing in Davies's court. In addition, Faubus's public criticism of Judge Davies and his filing, through his attorney, of a petition challenging the judge's authority raised doubts as to the governor's willingness to comply with federal court orders.[34]

At the trial on September 20 events moved toward a climax. After presenting their case, the governor's attorneys walked out of court. Justice Department lawyers then argued the sole issue of whether a possibility of violence was present on or before September 3. Their argument was unfortunate in that no effort was made to base it on the FBI's evidence that virtually no threat of violence existed. Moreover, the argument failed to develop the more fundamental point that if Faubus had resorted to police powers out of concern about potential disorder, his lawful course would have been to protect the constitutional rights of the black children by assisting the federal court in enforcing integration.[35] Despite the shortcomings of the Justice Department's argument, however, Judge Davies ruled against the governor and stressed that Faubus had erred in refusing to exercise police powers lawfully.[36] By this time, Faubus had removed the National Guard, leaving a vacuum in civil authority in Little Rock.

But the Justice Department's emphasis during the trial on potential violence had unwittingly established grounds for causing disruption, which would thereby seem to justify Governor Faubus's original use of troops.[37] This became apparent when school officials requested U.S. marshals to assist in the enforcement of integration on September 23. It was also a factor influencing the department's rejection of the school board's request and its decision that stronger measures were necessary. After discussions among Brownell, General Maxwell Taylor of the Joint Chiefs of Staff, and others, it was agreed that only regular troops could adequately defend the rights of the nine black children if disorder occurred as they entered Central. Brownell and Taylor reached this conclusion, they said, because they doubted the loyalty of federalized Arkansas National Guardsmen and considered deputization of large numbers of U.S. marshals "impractical." [38]

Once trouble developed on September 23 the federal government proceeded according to its preconceived plan. The following day Little Rock mayor W. W. Mann asked the president for assistance in a statement approved by White House aide Rabb; Brownell then notified President Eisenhower, who issued a proclamation prepared about a week earlier, ordering federal intervention in the city to preserve order and federal judicial authority. As the president made his statement, elements of the 101st Airborne were already on their way to Central. [39]

THE SCHOOL BOARD IMMOBILIZED

Legal principles, then, interacted with political exigencies to shape the decisions of Governor Faubus and the Justice Department. Little Rock school officials, buffeted by a similar interaction, proved incapable of taking any decisive action. The late 1956 and early 1957 Arkansas voter and general assembly approval of interposition measures had indirectly challenged the Phase Program. The challenge became more direct in March 1957 when segregationists campaigned for school board openings, embroiling the Blossom Plan in class tensions, gubernatorial politics, and uncertainty as to the legal basis of integration. Neither the appellate court's approval of the Phase Program in *Aaron* nor Faubus's assertion that integration was a local problem eased the board's concern. A. F. House's mission to Washington and local officials' exchanges with Justice Department attorney Caldwell during his fact-finding visit to Little Rock in June indicated the depth of uneasiness. But the board's concern did not result in a move to defuse the situation by independently pursuing a court injunction like that granted in Hoxie. In July Guthridge's suit on behalf of the dissatisfied parents of children attending Central further heightened pressure on the school administrators. [40]

In response to these and other developments Superintendent

Blossom had repeated discussions with local authorities and
Governor Faubus, but nothing seemed adequate to stimulate him
to take any initiatives. By mid-August school officials believed
a public pronouncement from Faubus was necessary to insure
against possible disruption of integration. Upton and Blossom
went so far as to consider a court test of the interposition measures as a means of encouraging the governor to make the
hoped-for statement, but they did not follow through on the
idea.[41] In the *Thomason* case, of course, Governor Faubus pursued the school board's litigation initiative to challenge rather
than support integration. The governor's privately sponsored
suit placed the school board in a difficult position. The narrow
legal issue in the case was whether a sufficient potential for
violence existed to warrant enjoining the scheduled start of integration at Central. The larger question for the school board
was whether the segregationists' summer activities constituted
a significant enough challenge to the Phase Program to justify
public scrutiny in court. Blossom's testimony admitting no general concern about disorder indicated that the board had decided against opening up the possibility of such an evaluation.[42]

After September 2 the school officials' weak-willed approach
created problems for them. When the school board asked Judge
Davies to postpone implementation of the Blossom Plan, it based
its request primarily on the fact of Faubus's obstructionism. Before considering a request for delay the judge, already con-
fronting a major constitutional issue concerning the legitimate
exercise of police powers, required a much fuller record of evidence than the school board was willing to present. In effect,
Blossom's testimony on August 29 had set the board on a course
that precluded presentation of such evidence. In addition, re-
quests for assistance from U.S. marshals conveyed to the judge
the impression that the school officials' thinking was confused.[43] The subsequent interplay of events precluded a clear-
ing up of the difficulties of the school board's position. Thus,
as had occurred in the *Thomason* suit, the trial of September 20
bound school officials to a perspective that incompletely conveyed the problems they confronted.[44]

The limits of this perspective became evident after President

Eisenhower's dispatch of U.S. armed forces to Little Rock. As the paratroopers established order, Superintendent Blossom urged the federal government to prosecute agitators in the crowd who had created trouble on September 23 and 24. Little Rock federal attorney Cobb responded to Blossom's request with an effort to prosecute eight ringleaders. Others in the Justice Department supported some form of action, though not necessarily that suggested by Cobb.[45] Following a visit to Little Rock, St. John Barrett of the Justice Department's Civil Rights Section reported to his superiors that local officials were "entitled to support from the Government. Any feeling on their part or on the part of other elements in the community that they were not receiving such support could very well abate their efforts to comply with the court's order." Furthermore, Barrett surmised, failure to act "might encourage persons . . . to interfere with" court-ordered integration.[46]

Despite these appeals, the new U.S. attorney general, William P. Rogers, declined to allow federal prosecution of the agitators. No doubt Rogers's decision was influenced by FBI director J. Edgar Hoover's resistance on grounds of procedural and policy considerations. Perhaps another factor was the intense criticism heaped upon the Eisenhower Administration for its use of paratroopers.[47] Harry Ashmore of the *Arkansas Gazette* speculated that refusal to prosecute was tied to Rogers's easy confirmation by the Senate Judiciary Committee "without a single question being addressed to him regarding his past or future course in the Little Rock case." Ashmore queried whether the committee's approval might not have involved "one of the most singular political deals in recent years."[48] Whatever the ultimate motives, the impact of the attorney general's order was that local authorities—particularly the school board—were left with responsibility for any legal action that might be taken against troublemakers. The board did not prosecute the agitators: Blossom insisted that such action was the duty of the federal government, not a school board.[49]

In and of itself Blossom's view had merit, but in a larger sense it reflected the unwillingness to take any public initiative that had characterized the board's policy throughout the summer. The board members accepted the proposition that litigation might be useful if brought by the NAACP, the segregationists, or someone else. But they would not take the initiative themselves, relying instead upon the private activities of mid-August. Thus the school board, which might have been able to prevent the fall confrontation by acting decisively during the summer, floundered impotently instead.[50]

THE AGONY OF THE NAACP

Ironically, the fourth principal in the drama—the local NAACP—was the only one actively seeking to play a responsible role, and circumstances conspired to deny it a successful part. The express purpose of the NAACP was the preservation of the constitutional rights of black people in Arkansas. During 1956, in *Aaron* v. *Cooper*, with little help or encouragement from the parent organization, the Little Rock branch worked to enable young blacks to attend integrated schools in the city. When the appellate court sustained the Phase Program in April 1957, the local NAACP shifted its legal efforts to the protection of the nine children who were to be enrolled at Central High School.[51] During the summer, however, the organization found it necessary to devote increased attention to fending off state-sponsored litigation aimed at disrupting its activities.[52] And once the crisis broke, much of its energies were consumed in defending its own right to exist.

During August the Little Rock branch initiated litigation challenging the recent segregationist legislation, only to become mired in a legal morass. In *Smith* v. *Faubus* ten black ministers asked the federal district court to declare the state's interposition measures unconstitutional and to issue a permanent injunction to prevent the state sovereignty commission from enforcing the 1957 laws. Governor Faubus, as official chairman of the commission, and eleven others were named as defendants. For more than a year, however, this litigation engaged the attention of the NAACP without being resolved. R. B. McCulloch, for the defendants, used procedural technicalities to move the *Smith* case from federal to state courts. Although McCulloch knew he would lose, throughout the fall and into the next year he labored with considerable skill to keep the case at issue but unresolved in order to buy time. As the *Smith* case dragged on indefinitely, the NAACP initiated further suits challenging the constitutionality of the sovereignty commission and other interposition measures, but each suit became entangled in a jungle of procedural intricacies.[53]

Meanwhile, the local NAACP had been thrown on the defensive on August 26, 1957, when Attorney General Bennett filed two suits in local chancery court under the new statutes imposing registration requirements and corporate franchise taxes on foreign corporations (those operating in Arkansas under out-of-state charters). The laws had as their object only civil rights organizations such as the Urban League and the NAACP. Bennett's two suits charged that the NAACP owed back taxes and had failed to comply with the new registration requirements. The central aim of the suits, however, was public revelation of records involving the internal operations of the NAACP and the names of its leaders and financial supporters.[54]

Attorney General Bennett was forthright in explaining the reasons for the registration and tax suits. "The turmoil and conflict between the races can be simply reduced to the amount of activity carried on by local branches of the NAACP," he said. "When the public knows who the local officers of the NAACP are, I think it will materially reduce their activities. With such reduction there will come peace and tranquility to the people of Arkansas again."[55] When the attorney general wrote to Mrs. L. C. Bates requesting detailed information, she and Rev. Crenchaw were prepared. Bates replied as "a citizen of Arkansas" desiring "to cooperate with lawful authorities" and gave some data demanded under the new laws. Other information involving legal counsel and financial donors was, she said, "privileged under freedom of speech and assembly guarantees of the Fourteenth Amendment and . . . the . . . Constitution." Furthermore, she concluded, given the "current climate of opinion" in the state, such revelations would lead to reprisals.[56]

This response led to litigation and an order for the arrest of Bates and Crenchaw. Both NAACP leaders voluntarily appeared at the Little Rock police station, were booked, paid a bond, and were released pending trial. At the same time, George

Howard and other local NAACP attorneys began litigation aimed at overturning the laws under which the two leaders were arrested. After some procedural maneuvering in federal and state court, federal judge Ray W. Harper and chancery judge Murray O. Reed agreed to a compromise by which Mrs. Bates and Rev. Crenchaw would remain free until the constitutionality of the so-called Bennett laws was determined. Since these laws were tied up in court indefinitely, Bennett's efforts at prosecution came to naught.[57]

As local NAACP leaders became increasingly involved in defending themselves, Wiley Branton and other Legal Defense Fund lawyers, notably Thurgood Marshall, took a steadily more important part in the fight. Marshall had appeared with Branton during the spring appeal of *Aaron*, and the two represented the black children's rights in litigation spawned by the *Thomason* suit. On August 30, and each time thereafter when the school board went to Judge Davies requesting direction or a delay, Branton (and usually Marshall) was there to argue for continuance of the Phase Program sustained in *Aaron* v. *Cooper*. New York-based LDF lawyers assisted in the litigation over the Bennett laws, and they also participated in the September 20 trial of Governor Faubus.[58] Apparently due to their periodic negotiations with the governor, the Justice Department "went to great length" to get the LDF to withdraw from its commitment to the integration of Central. The LDF staff did not, however, cooperate with the department on this issue.[59]

But it was not until Faubus's proclamation made international news that the New York office of the NAACP virtually took over the cause in Little Rock. After September 3 continuous telephone communication (funded outside Arkansas) was established between Little Rock and national headquarters. Early in the fall of 1957 Clarence A. Laws replaced Frank Smith as field secretary; by phone and letter he kept in regular touch with the New York leadership, while directly assisting Bates, Crenchaw, and others in local matters. Understandably, local and national considerations of policy became one, as everyone worked to protect the welfare of the nine children attending Central as well as to cooperate with the media, the federal government, and innumerable visitors.[60]

One indication of the Little Rock branch's adjustment to its new role involved Dr. Lee Lorch. Lorch and his wife had rendered invaluable and dedicated service to the cause of racial justice in the capital city. No doubt due to this activity, their home was the object of an unsuccessful dynamite plant. Even so, the couple's known Communist affiliations created problems for the NAACP's moderate image.[61] By November 1957, field secretary Laws felt compelled to write to Lorch. Noting the professor's "unauthorized" calls to members of the city council concerning actions against the NAACP, Laws sought "to make a number of things crystal clear." The field secretary asserted that integration in Little Rock "could be done irreparable harm by the injection of extraneous issues." He then expressed the view that the "best contribution" Lorch "could make to the cause of full citizenship for Negroes in Arkansas . . . would be to terminate, in writing," his affiliation with the Little Rock branch of the NAACP. By the end of 1958 the Lorches had moved to Canada.[62]

The events of the fall of 1957 in Little Rock were dramatic. Attracting public attention at first were Governor Faubus's states' rights stand, the embattled school board, a timid federal government, and the beleaguered NAACP. After September 24 President Eisenhower's direct intervention and the plight of the nine black children overshadowed earlier developments. Obscured by the drama, however, were vital constitutional issues which shaped the actions of protagonists. The segregationists' formulation of the doctrine of police powers pushed the governor into a difficult political position. The school board's private August initiative, considered in the context of its legalistic rationale for integration, no doubt influenced Faubus's ultimate decision to defy federal authority in order to avoid responsibility for implementation of the Phase Program. The force of constitutional principle also limited the Justice Department's procedural and policy choices. Only the NAACP championed unqualified obedience to the rule established in *Brown*, and external harassment and internal organizational adjustment constricted its effectiveness. As a result of these factors the constitutional issues were deferred, not resolved.

NOTES

1. Military Powers of the Executive as Related to the Courts," 2 *Race Relations Law Reporter* 1071 (1957), provides a thorough review of judicial precedents and periodical literature relating to police powers of chief executives. James Jackson Kilpatrick, "A Virginia Editor: Some Conflicting Rights," in Wilson Record and Jane Cassels Record, eds., *Little Rock, U.S.A.* (San Francisco, 1960), 231–236, gives an analysis of police powers justifying Governor Faubus's actions by ignoring the full scope of precedents and issues.

2. "Military Powers," 2 *RRLR* 1071 (1957).

3. Brooks Hays, *A Southern Moderate Speaks* (Chapel Hill, 1959), 155–156. For fuller treatment see John C. Calhoun, "Disquisition on Government," in *Works of John C. Calhoun*, 4 vols. (New York, 1863), vol. 1, especially 15, 16, 25.

4. *Moyer* v. *Peabody*, 212 U.S. 78, 85–86 (1909). See also "Military Powers," 2 *RRLR* 1071 (1957).

5. *Sterling* v. *Constantin*, 287 U.S. 378, 400–401 (1932).

6. Ibid., 402–404. See also "Military Powers," 2 *RRLR* 1071 (1957).

7. *Strutwear Knitting Co.* v. *Olson*, 13 F. Supp. 384, 390, 391 (D.C. Minn. 1936).

8. In "The Story of Little Rock—As Governor Faubus Tells It," *U.S. News & World Report*, June 20, 1958, 102, Faubus expressed his view of this issue, which ran contrary to the federal decisions just cited, but also suggested the extent to which his own political standing was a crucial consideration. If he had used the Guard to protect black children entering Central and to enforce a federal court order the "people would have been enemies of the Guard and enemies of mine. . . . If it's . . . a federal [court order]—which it isn't—let the federal agents enforce it."

9. "Injunction against Governor [Faubus]," 2 *RRLR* 957, 962 (1957).

10. *Faubus* v. *U.S.*, 3 *RRLR* 439, 446 (U.S.C.A. 8th Cir. 1958), citing *Sterling* v. *Constantin*, 287 U.S. 378, 397 (1932).

11. Faubus, *Down from the Hills*, 206–207, makes such an argument.

12. *Crisis in the South: The Little Rock Story* (Little Rock, 1958), 26, connects Faubus's desire for a third term with his igniting of the crisis in September. Faubus, *Down from the Hills*, especially 206, contends that he saw no political advantage, but rather an uncertain political consequence for the action. That Faubus acted out of uncertainty as to the ultimate political ramifications is essentially the point of Numan V. Bartley, "Looking Back at Little Rock," *Arkansas Historical Quarterly*, 25 (Summer 1966), 101–116. See also note 24 below, and Elliff, "Department of Justice," 469.

13. My argument follows Professor Bartley, except that I believe the data found in the FBI report and other sources cited in chap. 4 support the extension presented here and below.

14. Bartley, "Looking Back," 101–116. Elliff, "Department of Justice," 469. Faubus, *Down from the Hills*, 169.

15. Given the extent of the governor's activities involving integration—concerning not only communications with school officials, but the July meeting with segregationist leaders—the actual impact of Griffin's speech needs to be reconsidered. Although Faubus may have detected a "change in mood" regarding the community's acceptance of integration after Griffin's speech, as he said in his September 2 proclamation, he had already done enough to suggest that he was preparing for as many conceivable contingencies as possible, even if Griffin had not come to Little Rock. Note, too, that the controversy over appointments to the state sovereignty commission was a significant part of the governor's maneuvering. Memo, Arthur B. Caldwell to Warren Olney III, Aug. 30, 1957, "Conference with Governor of Arkansas, August 28, 1957," #144–100–9, ABCP (UAF), suggests that Faubus delayed making appointments to the commission so that they could not be tested in court. Interview with L. R. Luker, in FBI Report 44–12285–855, shows, however, that the governor made his appointments only after a segregationist from East Arkansas, who had been lobbying for a seat, filed a chancery court suit ordering the governor to act. The segregationist filed the suit, he said, to "force" Faubus to make the appointments, which he did within a matter of days. Osro Cobb, "*United States* v. *Governor Orval E. Faubus et Al.*" (manuscript, UALR, A, n.d.), notes that Faubus delayed in making appointments in order to "keep people guessing" as to his stand on integration. Several other factors support these conclusions. For example, the Amis Guthridge interview, DDEP (1972), 1–30, states that segregationists were distrustful of and uncertain about Faubus's actions as the Sept. 3 opening of Central neared. This was suggested by Governor Griffin's query upon hearing of Faubus's use of the National Guard: did he call them out "for or a'gin us?" Despite frequent contacts, neither Blossom nor the school board knew where Faubus stood, though school officials had told the governor privately that they would not file a suit challenging the constitutionality of the 1957 interposition legislation and were aware that he was considering private sponsorship of such a suit himself (see memo, Caldwell to Olney, Aug. 30, 1957; and Blossom, *It Has Happened Here*, 52–54, 60–61). Faubus of course was aware of the school board's aborted decision to pursue litigation and knew about the *Wilburn* suit. But he apparently did not know whether the school board and the Justice Department were making secret preparations for

the opening of Central. Also, as his private conference with Caldwell
suggested, he had hopes, until the day before the trial of *Thomason*,
that the federal government would intervene. See also Faubus, *Down
from the Hills*, 199–204.

16. Memo, Caldwell to Olney, Aug. 30, 1957; and Faubus, *Down from
the Hills*, 206.

17. In W. J. Smith, interview with author, Sept. 3, 1980, Mr. Smith
noted that the governor acknowledged a duty to obey final court orders as a result of his (Smith's) advice. John Thomas Elliff, "The United
States, Department of Justice and Individual Rights, 1937–1962" (Ph.D.
diss., Harvard University, 1967), 472–477.

18. Arthur B. Caldwell to Warren Olney III, July 24, 1957, "Segregation in Public Schools in Arkansas," #144–100–9, ABCP (UAF).

19. Ibid.

20. Memo, Caldwell to Olney, Aug. 30, 1957. Elliff, "Department of
Justice," 463, 485. See also Faubus, *Down from the Hills*, 197–199, for a
somewhat different view. Section 241, Title 18 is the portion of the U.S.
Code referred to in the text.

21. Elliff, "Department of Justice," 466.

22. Ibid., 466–467.

23. Ibid., 468–469. For another view, without benefit of private Justice Department memos, see Blossom, *It Has Happened Here*, 85–98. See
also the school board's Sept. 3 request for instructions and the Sept. 5
petition for a stay of integration and Judge Davies's orders of Sept. 3
and Sept. 7 in 2 *RRLR* 937–941. See also *SSN*, Oct. 1957, 2–5.

24. A large portion of FBI Report 44–12284–933 is devoted to interviews with, and a review of the records of, some one hundred stores
(perhaps every one in Little Rock and North Little Rock) where guns,
knives, and other weapons of the sort mentioned in Governor Faubus's Sept. 2 proclamation might have been obtained. The report
showed conclusively that there was "no significant increase" in sales
during the summer as compared with earlier months or years, and that
the sales that were made were not of a suspicious nature. Every other
statement by the governor justifying his concern about trouble was
checked and rechecked with similar thoroughness, leading to the same
result. A check of "evidence" presented by W. J. Smith supported the
same conclusion. Interestingly, the FBI report does document Blossom's various statements of concern and the Upton initiative involving Judge Miller. This evidence was never addressed by Justice Department representatives, as far as I can determine. See also Warren
Olney, "Summary of FBI Report in Little Rock, Arkansas Integration
Difficulty," Sept. 13, 1957, #144–100–9, ABCP (UAF).

25. Elliff, "Department of Justice," 469.

26. Ibid., 469–470.
27. Ibid., 470–471.
28. Ibid., 471–472.
29. Ibid., 472. Elliff notes that, despite the cautious approach, the Justice Department was nonetheless going beyond limits established in the Hoxie and Clinton precedents.
30. Ibid., 473–474.
31. Ibid.
32. 2 *RRLR* 1077–1078 (1957).
33. Ibid.
34. Ibid., 475. For text of the petition challenging Davies's authority, see 2 *RRLR* 943–957.
35. Elliff, "Department of Justice," 476–477.
36. 2 *RRLR* 957–963.
37. Elliff, "Department of Justice," 476–477. J. W. Peltason, *Fifty-Eight Lonely Men: Southern Federal Judges and School Desegregation* (New York, 1961), 173.
38. Elliff, "Department of Justice," 477–478.
39. Ibid., 479.
40. See chap. 4, specifically sections noting mounting tension prior to and including the climax of August 1957.
41. See chap. 4, notes 51–53.
42. The governor knew, of course, that school board members had decided against involvement in a suit testing the constitutionality of the 1957 interposition measures. See memo, Caldwell to Olney, Aug. 30, 1957.
43. *SSN*, Oct. 1957, 1–30 Blossom, *It Has Happened Here*, 89.
44. Failure to make public the FBI report also aided Governor Faubus in his efforts to justify his stand; "Story of Little Rock," 106. See also chap. 6.
45. Elliff, "Department of Justice," 479–485. Cobb, "*U.S.* v. *Faubus.*"
46. Elliff, "Department of Justice," 481.
47. Elliff states that Rogers's replacement of Brownell as attorney general was due to the latter's decision made early in the fall. Ibid., 483. For Hoover's role see Ibid., 484. For the level of criticism see chap. 6.
48. Elliff, "Department of Justice," 484–485.
49. Ibid., 483–484.
50. Caldwell to Olney, July 24, 1957, "Segregation in Public Schools in Arkansas," ABCP (UAF). Elliff, "Department of Justice," 407–420, goes into great detail, relying upon private Justice Department memos and letters about *Hoxie*.

51. This shift is noted in Wiley Branton interview, DDEP (1973); and in Wiley Branton, interview with author, Dec. 11, 1979.

52. *SSN*, Sept. 1957, 6; *Smith* v. *Faubus*, 2 *RRLR* 1103 (U.S.C.A. 8th Cir. 1957); Elliff, "Department of Justice," 429–433. See also chap. 2.

53. *SSN*, Dec. 1957, 2, 3; Jan. 1958, 8, 9; Feb. 1958, 12; Apr. 1958, 12; May 1958, 6.

54. *SSN*, Sept. 1957, 2. "State Sovereignty Commission and Case Against Governor, et al.," FBI Report 44–12284–933. For details of Attorney General Bennett's program, see below. See also *Arkansas* v. *NAACP*, complaint filed in circuit court, Pulaski County, DBP (SHSW, AD), Box 6, Folder 4, MS. 523.

55. "Excerpts from a speech delivered by Bruce Bennett to a Civic Club at El Dorado, Arkansas, on Oct. 9, 1957." See also Bennett to Mayor W. W. Mann, Oct. 9, 1957, DBP (SHSW, AD), Box 6, Folder 4, MS. 523.

56. Bruce Bennett to Mrs. Daisy Bates, Aug. 30, 1957; Bates to Bennett, Sept. 13, 1957, DBP (SHSW, AD), Box 6, Folder 4, MS. 523. See also W. W. Mann to Bates, Oct. 15, 1957 (same source). Another source used here, located in DBP (SHSW, AD), Folder 2, Box 5, are transcripts of phone conversations between Mrs. Bates and officers in the New York headquarters of the NAACP from Sept. 25, 1957, to Nov. 13, 1957. These transcripts while useful for specific information, are also revealing in a general way about how New York headquarters became oriented to Little Rock as a center of civil rights struggle.

57. See *SSN*, Sept. 1957, 2, for narrative of public record. The phone transcripts (cited in note 56 above) for Oct. 11, Oct. 23, Nov. 1, and Nov. 4, 1957, give internal NAACP strategy. Robert L. Carter (General Counsel, NAACP LDF), to George Howard, Jr., Oct. 23, 1957, DBP (SHSW, AD), Box 4, gives details on procedural strategy.

58. Bates, *Long Shadow*, 57, 83. Branton interview, DDEP (1973); Branton, interview with author, Dec. 11, 1979. Phone transcripts Sept. 25, 1957, to Nov. 13, 1957, DBP (SHSW, AD), Box 5, Folder 2. Cobb, "*U.S.* v. *Faubus*."

59. Branton interview, DDEP (1973); Branton, interview with author, Dec. 11, 1979.

60. Phone transcripts make clear how unaware the New York NAACP was of the developments in Little Rock prior to September 3. It is useful to compare these transcripts and the "educational process" they represent for NAACP headquarters with the story of the *Aaron* v. *Cooper* litigation, chap. 2. Concerning Laws's replacement of Smith see transcripts for Oct. 4, 1957; and Frank Smith, "Field Secretary's Report to the Executive Board," Oct. 26, 1957, DBP (SHSW, AD), Box 4, MS. 523. For the public record of issues not treated here, particularly the

story of the nine children at Central and the NAACP's role, see Bates, *Long Shadow*.

61. Lee Lorch to L. C. Bates, Sept. 12, 1959, DBP (SHSW, AD) Box 5, Folder 9, MS. 523; and phone transcript Nov. 1, 1957, DBP (SHSW, AD), Box 5, Folder 2.

62. Clarence A. Laws to Dr. Lee Lorch, Nov. 1, 1957, DBP (SHSW, AD), Box 4, MS. 523. See also Lorch to Bates, Sept. 12, 1959.

The Crisis
Resolved _____ 6

From late 1957 to the fall of 1958 conditions in Little Rock declined from deadlock to intractable confrontation. Governor Faubus, the school board, the Justice Department, segregationists, and the NAACP remained the principal actors in the drama, though in August the United States Supreme Court also became directly involved for the first time. The Court's intervention intensified rather than eased the struggle, as state authorities moved to close the city's public high schools for 1958–1959. In the face of such recalcitrance, a reassertion of local moderate business and civic leadership, building upon federal judicial authority, brought an end to the conflict.

DEADLOCK: 1957–1958

In November 1957 Little Rock seemed immobilized. A "near stalemate" prevailed at Central High School, where U.S. military personnel patrolled hallways and grounds. School administrators wrestled with problems arising from the harassment of the nine black young people by a handful of segregationist-supported student troublemakers. At the same time, most students within the school remained neutral.[1] In the capital city itself business activity slowed, as segregationists threatened and eventually implemented a boycott of businesses owned or operated by moderates or supporters of integration. Moreover, after years of steady industrial development new industries abruptly stopped moving into the community.[2] Defeated in the lower court, segregationists appealed cases challenging the constitutionality of President Eisenhower's use of troops and of the Phase Program itself; but no decision was expected in these suits until the spring of 1958. Attorney General Bennett's cases against the NAACP and the organization's own efforts at overturning interposition measures also made little progress.[3] Finally, before the new year, segregationists began demanding a special August term of the legislature to deal with the deadlock.[4]

There were other indications of an electric calm. Election of candidates for the new city manager form of government became embroiled in the desegregation conflict. Moderate civic leaders had led the move toward a new municipal government system, which had made Mayor Mann a lame duck during the crisis. Unexpectedly, in the November elections segregationists gave moderate candidates close and heated competition, though the traditional coalition of black and high-income white wards gave moderates a narrow victory. Further tension arose from charges of Communist activity in Little Rock, arising out of federal and state investigations of Mrs. Grace Lorch.[5] Meanwhile, efforts by two groups—a committee of southern state governors and a group of moderate Little Rock businessmen led by Walter C. Guy—to negotiate a compromise and a withdrawal of the troops proved futile.[6] In Washington, Senator John Stennis of the Judiciary Committee tried to prevent the allocation of funds to support the federal government's presence in Little Rock; but that, too, failed.[7]

Federal authorities, Governor Faubus, and the school board responded in different ways to the stalemate. After deciding against prosecution of rabble rousers in the disorders of September 23 and 24, the Justice Department "virtually retired" from Little Rock.[8] Judge Davies remained in the city on special assignment (which was scheduled to end in March, 1958), and he joined other federal judges in special three-member tribunals to hear the Bennett and NAACP cases; but he was less regularly criticized during the winter than he had been during the early fall.[9] The vacant judgeship itself, however, was the object of continued controversy, as civic leaders called on the federal government and their elected officials in Washington to appoint someone with awareness of and kinship with "regional values." Governor Faubus and segregationists aggravated the situation further by charging that the federal government's slowness in making an appointment reflected a conspiracy that had set off the September crisis.[10]

As 1957 ended the Little Rock school board became even more demoralized. The extent of the board's troubles was suggested by the breakup of the attorney group formed by Superintendent Blossom in 1956. On September 4 Leon Catlett wrote to Blossom that he considered he had "fully discharged" his obligations to school officials.[11] By December two other attorneys had withdrawn from the group, leaving only Richard Butler to assist A. F. House in the school board's legal defense. The size and extensive federal practice of the firms to which House and Butler belonged perhaps influenced their decision to stay with the board's cause, and both lawyers believed that preservation of quality education in Little Rock depended upon dissolving the deadlock within the city. Neither, however, was sure of how best to achieve this goal.[12]

As the stalemate dragged on Governor Faubus became increasingly identified with the segregationists and grew in popularity as a result. In November and December observers found the governor's political standing among Arkansans to be higher than ever. There was a growing expectation that he would announce his candidacy for a third gubernatorial term, though Faubus himself made no public commitment. While he worked vigorously to carry out his developmental program, Faubus also often discussed the fall crisis and desegregation in general. As it became clear that the federal government would prosecute no one for the September disorders, he took an increasingly explicit segregationist stand. Playing to public bitterness over the military presence in Little Rock, the governor criticized the federal government's creation of a new "police state," and attacked the United States Supreme Court. He also drew closer to segregationists themselves by paying attention to demands for a special assembly session and noting the supposed threat of Communism. Echoing segregationist contentions, he said, "I can see no other alternative [to continued trouble] than a voluntary withdrawal of those [nine black] children."[13]

Following the New Year, activity in Little Rock quickened. Disruptive incidents continued to occur at Central and throughout the city. After a rock shattered a window in the home of Mr. and Mrs. L. C. Bates, police were assigned to protect the couple. Similar arrangements had already been made for school officials and others publicly involved with desegregation.[14] Amidst these developments, the school board came under mounting pressure to seek a postponement of the Phase Program.[15] In January 1958 Amis Guthridge called upon the board to follow the example of New Orleans school authorities who had sought a delay during desegregation litigation in the Crescent City, and Governor Faubus and Jim Johnson publicly asserted new positions on desegregation.[16] Johnson's position rested on a proposed constitutional amendment which, among other provisions, would strengthen the state sovereignty commission and provide for the closing of schools and the selling of their property whenever integration occurred in a community without a majority vote. Faubus, in keeping with his steady movement toward a hard-line segregationist stance since late September, articulated a position similar to that of his old opponent, proposing that a popular vote in each school district should decide the issue of desegregation.[17]

Amidst these developments, on January 18 school board member R. A. Lile wrote privately to President Eisenhower. Lile suggested that a conference attended by himself, Superintendent Blossom, the president, and others would present important new facts which could "throw some light . . . on the question of *Where do we go from here?*" Members of the White House staff, representatives of the Justice Department, and Attorney General Rogers discussed Lile's proposal, but even though there was some sentiment favoring a conference, Rogers decided against it. The department's Office of Legal Counsel responded to the board member that while Little Rock's case was still in litigation, it was "neither advisable nor appropriate for the Executive to inject himself into it or to confer with anyone outside the Government regarding it at this particular time."[18]

In the face of the Eisenhower administration's continued refusal to provide active support for integration, even moderates in Little Rock decided that it was best to postpone the implementation of the Phase Program. In February Walter C. Guy's committee publicly recommended that the school board risk a delay on the ground that many citizens who "believe in law and order . . . are not satisfied that all the legal avenues open to us have been fully explored, especially in the light of our experiences of the past several months." The next day the school board filed a petition in federal district court requesting a postponement. The petition summarized the record of the Phase Program from its inception to the troubles of 1957–1958, noted the failure of federal authorities to support local efforts to comply with *Brown*, and stressed the extent to which interposition measures and statements by state officials had fostered public confusion over the constitutional basis of desegregation in Little Rock. All this left the school board "standing alone, the victim of extraordinary opposition on the part of the state government and apathy on the part of the federal government." [19] In light of these considerations, the board requested a delay until the courts determined the application in Little Rock of the concept of "all deliberate speed." [20]

The school board's petition put the federal government on the spot. The Justice Department, for its part, continued to duck responsibility in this new stage of the *Aaron* litigation; consistent with the earlier pattern, department officials decided against doing anything. [21] But the new litigation raised still another problem for federal authorities. Because of the vacancy created by Judge Trimble's retirement, it was unclear who would hear the school board's case. Given the criticism of Judge Davies as a "foreigner" during the fall, his presiding in the suit seemed ill advised. Thus, on the day the school board attorneys filed their petition, the Justice Department announced that its preference for Trimble's replacement was J. Smith Henley, a department attorney and a native of the Ozark Mountain region of northwestern Arkansas. No one could tell, however, how quickly the Senate would decide upon confirmation, especially after his selection aroused criticism within Arkansas. [22]

In spring pressure on the moderates was intensified by Faubus's announcement of his candidacy for a third term and by his now unequivocal segregationist position. He did say that his developmental program was still an important issue, but he declared that integration and states' rights would constitute the major focus of his campaign. As other candidates filed, the governor struck an increasingly demagogic segregationist stance.[23] In May 1958 he said that troops could become necessary again if blacks tried for readmission to Central High, and he suggested that a special legislative session in August might be necessary to consider closing any school where federal troops were used to enforce desegregation.[24] When a former Justice Department attorney revealed in a public statement that the governor had sponsored the *Thomason* suit during the last week in August 1957, Faubus denied having had any involvement in the case.[25] What was more, Faubus reversed his earlier position—that federal court decisions were binding as the "law of the land"—and now argued that the Supreme Court's decisions were not valid expressions of national law. Only Congress or "the people," he contended, could make such law.[26]

Governor Faubus's proclamation of an expressly segregationist legal argument followed a rejection of these arguments by the federal appellate court. The U.S. Eighth Circuit Court denied the governor's claim that the police powers had sanctioned the obstruction of desegregation on September 3. Following established precedents, the circuit court held that no resort to the police powers could justify a deprivation of constitutional rights.[27] The court also refused to accept two other segregationist claims. In an appeal of the *Thomason* case, the court upheld Judge Davies's judgment in reversing the chancery court decision of August 29, 1957, enjoining the school board's implementation of its Phase Program.[28] At the same time, the court rejected a petition challenging the constitutionality of President Eisenhower's use of U.S. military personnel, holding that there was no substantial constitutional question concerning the action of the president.[29]

Like Governor Faubus, segregationists took their discredited legal claims to the voters. Amis Guthridge filed against Brooks Hays in the race for the U.S. House of Representatives, and Jim Johnson campaigned for a seat on the Arkansas Supreme Court. While not seeking office himself, Reverend Pruden called for legislation that would permit recall of local school board members.[30]

In this heated political context a federal judge was named to hear the school board's petition for delay. In accord with the "public interest," Chief Judge Archibald Gardner of the Eighth Circuit Court of Appeals chose federal district judge Harry J. Lemley to preside over the case.[31] For years Judge Lemley had lived and practiced law in the southwestern Arkansas town of Hope. In 1939 President Roosevelt had appointed him to the federal bench; in 1958 he was seventy-four years old and had established a solid record as a diligent judge in the federal district of Southwest Arkansas. Lemley was also something of a scholar; he had published on the archeology of Arkansas Indian mounds and done research toward a history of the Confederacy.[32] It was said of him that he loved the South "almost as a religion," but he had dealt fairly with the few integration cases that had come before him.[33] Once involved in the Little Rock litigation, he admitted privately to U.S. Attorney Cobb that the level of disruption of the educational process at Central was "shocking," but otherwise there were no clues to how he would decide the case.[34]

THE SUPREME COURT INTERVENES

During the summer of 1958 events moved toward another confrontation. Early in June Judge Lemley heard final arguments in the *Cooper* v. *Aaron* litigation and announced that the granting of a postponement would depend upon the persuasiveness of the school board's evidence. Furthermore, he ordered the board's attorneys to amend their petition by specifying a precise date by which integration would be resumed if a delay were granted. House and Butler (with the help of John Haley, a young lawyer in House's firm), responded by preparing a detailed record of disorderly incidents occurring within Central. The record demonstrated extensive disruption of the school's ordinarily excellent academic program. The attorneys requested a delay of two and a half years.[35] NAACP lawyers, in rebuttal, argued that under principles established in *Brown* neither actual nor perceived disorder provided a basis for postponement of integration. When NAACP counsel asked board member Upton why school officials had selected two and a half

years as the period of delay, he replied that it was hoped that
by then Governor Faubus would no longer hold office. This admission, one newspaper noted, assured Faubus of a third-term
nomination in the upcoming primary.[36]

As the suit progressed, the Justice Department reconsidered
filing a petition for an injunction against segregationist leaders.
One department official wrote to Attorney General Rogers that
"the evidence now in hand is sufficient to warrant an injunction being issued." Ultimately, however, the department remained cautious, preferring to wait for action by the federal
courts. We, "of course," the official continued, "do not intend
at this time to make any suggestion whatever that the government should file an injunction complaint. We will, however, be
ready to move on very short notice if as a result of the hearings
the court should call in the United States Attorney."[37]

On June 21 Judge Lemley granted the board's petition for a
postponement. Emphasizing the need to preserve educational
quality, the judge termed his decision a "tactical delay" rather
than a surrender. He noted, too, that black children possessed
good educational facilities in the new Horace Mann High School
and in other schools in Little Rock.[38] The school board and the
city's moderates applauded the opinion; Faubus called it a "step
in the right direction."[39] But immediately NAACP attorneys
appealed both to the United States Circuit Court of Appeals and
the United States Supreme Court. Pointing out that simultane-
ous appeal was irregular, the Supreme Court declined to hear
the case until it was considered by the court of appeals. In his
order, however, Justice Felix Frankfurter emphasized the importance of immediate action in the lower court.[40]

Early in July 1958, as the court of appeals prepared to hear
the Little Rock case in a special session, the Justice Department
again discussed its position in light of Lemley's "unexpected"
decision. Should the department—on its own initiative—file an
amicus curiae (friend of the court) brief in the appellate court?
The NAACP brought pressure on the department to do so.
Thurgood Marshall had complained about the federal government's non-intervention, and by July 8 the Justice Department
had received 108 telegrams from NAACP branches across the
country. Department officials did prepare a petition and or-

dered another FBI investigation in the Arkansas capital, but other than "closely following all developments in the . . . litigation" it still declined to take direct action.[41]

The results of the primary elections in July also put pressure on the department to intervene: Faubus won the Democratic nomination—tantamount to election—in a landslide. Officials in Washington must have been bewildered by the fact that blacks in Little Rock and across the state voted overwhelmingly for Faubus, presumably because of his impressive record of accomplishments in improving Arkansas's economy and social services. What was most evident was that Arkansans of both races had apparently endorsed segregation, for in his campaign Faubus had appealed to the emotions, fears, and prejudices that had been aroused among whites since the preceding fall. Governor Faubus praised Judge Lemley's decision in *Cooper* v. *Aaron*, but stressed the threat of reversal by the federal court of appeals. Another indication of the high level of voter emotion in the primary was that Jim Johnson was elected to the Arkansas Supreme Court (though Guthridge was defeated in his bid to unseat Congressman Brooks Hays). If the appellate judges reversed Lemley's ruling, the governor's calling of a special legislative session seemed virtually certain, and that would intensify further the Justice Department's already difficult position.[42]

The circuit court's decision clouded rather than cleared the issue. On August 18 the court, by a six-to-one vote, overruled Judge Lemley's decision, holding that impending violence and related "administrative problems" did not remove from the school board a duty to adhere to the Constitution. But Chief Judge Gardner, the court's lone dissenter, delayed immediate implementation of the order until the Supreme Court could hear an appeal.[43] Faced with the circuit court's holding, the Justice Department initially considered filing a petition for an injunction against the segregationists. Attorney General Rogers went so far as to order three department lawyers to Little Rock to help local federal authorities in preparing the government's entry into the *Cooper* litigation. When Chief Judge Gardner granted the temporary delay, however, the department waited to act.[44] NAACP lawyers appealed to the Supreme Court.

Confronted with the rush of events, Chief Justice Earl Warren moved decisively. The Supreme Court's official term was
not scheduled to begin until October 6, but upon receiving the
NAACP's appeal Warren and his colleagues considered another procedure. Justice Charles E. Whittaker flew from Kansas
City to Los Angeles to confer with Justice William J. Brennan,
and then both flew to Washington. Justice Harold Burton prepared to cut short a trip to Europe to return to the nation's capital. Finally, the justices agreed that *Cooper* v. *Aaron* was significant enough to warrant calling a special term (only the third
such term in the modern history of the Court). Warren announced the Court's action on August 25; at the same time he
asked the federal government to participate in the litigation as
amicus curiae.[45]

The Court's resort to the special term generated criticism and
resistance. At the annual convention of state chief justices in
late August a majority of the state judges supported a resolution that "too often [the Supreme Court] has tended to adopt
the role of policy maker without proper judicial restraint."[46]
Governor Faubus responded by calling into special session the
Arkansas legislature to "deal with the problem." On August 26,
the assembly passed numerous bills giving the governor a wide
range of authority to prevent integration. But the central purpose of most of the measures was to establish a legal basis for
closing any public schools under court order to desegregate and
to transfer public funds to private, segregated institutions. Once
the governor signed the bills, he would have the power to temporarily close schools until voters expressed their will in a referendum. Faubus had called for these measures in an address
opening the special session; in supporting them he embraced
policies that Jim Johnson and other segregationists had argued
for since 1956. Other legislation (which was not part of the governor's package) gave the state attorney general a variety of
powers aimed at harassing the NAACP. After their passage,
Faubus waited before signing any of the bills into law.[47]

The Supreme Court's special term convened on August 28.
After hearing the school board's oral argument for an appeal
and the NAACP's rebuttal, the Court gave the parties until
September 7 to prepare briefs, and set September 11 for the full

hearing of the case. During the interim Little Rock school officials attempted to counter the governor's possible closing of
schools by delaying the beginning of the academic year until
September 15.[48] The Justice Department also considered its op-
tions prior to the September 11 hearing. Chief Justice Warren's
request for the government's participation seemed to resolve
months of vacillation within the department over whether to
involve itself in the newest stage of the Little Rock confrontation.[49] But it soon became apparent that indecision persisted.

Justice Department officials were still unable to agree on filing an injunction petition against the segregationists. The issue
involved whether the department should file the petition *before*
Central High opened and *prior to* any disorder. Complicating
the question were the school closing measures recently passed
by the Arkansas legislature. As department attorney Donald
MacGuines said, "In view of the fact that the opening of Central High School has been postponed and seems likely to be
postponed further in the light of action by the Arkansas Governor and Legislature, it seems unlikely that there will be any
objectionable action [by segregationists] . . . in the immediate
future." MacGuines therefore advised against injunctive proceedings "unless and until Central High School opens and there
is some real indication of current obstruction to the integration
plan."[50]

The question of independent initiative in Little Rock had be-
deviled the Justice Department since Arthur B. Caldwell's report of June 1957. During the interim before the Supreme Court's
hearing of September 11, the Justice Department attempted to
resolve this issue. Attorney General Rogers took steps to prepare a special team of United States marshals trained in riot
control. At the same time, lawyers in the department's Office
of Legal Counsel prepared legal memoranda supporting the use
of marshals and the appointment of local police officers as dep-
uty marshals. In addition, the legal office's attorneys set out the
attorney general's authority to use such forces "without prior
order" and the Justice Department's power to request a *Hoxie*-
type injunction "on its own initiative" against anyone interfering with integration in Little Rock. On the last point especially,
the office articulated a strong legal and constitutional rationale

for federal governmental authority to "proceed independently." Finally, the lawyers determined that the Arkansas legislature's school closing and private school measures were unconstitutional.[51]

Thus, by early September Rogers had clear constitutional authority for several avenues of independent action and seemed
ready to move at last. On September 7 he wrote letters to Little
Rock's city manager and school board informing them of the
availability of the specially trained U.S. marshals.[52] In the letter
to school board president Cooper the attorney general also noted
that if the Supreme Court upheld the overruling of Judge Lemley's decision, the board could ask for a *Hoxie*-like injunction to
forestall "an outbreak of violence." Rogers assured Cooper that
the Justice Department was prepared to "assist in any way which
may be helpful . . . in making the suggested application to"
the local federal district court. Rogers then ordered the marshals to Little Rock on September 11 but took no other independent legal initiative. After "careful consideration" of the
school board's decision, the Justice Department also declined
to initiate injunctive proceedings.[53]

The justices of the Supreme Court did not at first agree on
an appropriate response to the most recent developments in the
Little Rock case. Their views were of course not publicly known,
but they provide useful perspective on the justices' thinking just
prior to the hearing of September 11. For Chief Justice Warren
the case was apparently nothing less than a struggle between
the governor of Arkansas and the Supreme Court of the United
States. Justice Tom C. Clark, on the other hand, had so many
doubts about the special term that he considered dissenting from
the whole idea, and at least twice he drafted handwritten dissents. Clark did not "in any respect whatsoever" want to suggest that he desired to make "a change in position from that
taken in *Brown*. I adhere steadfastly to my vote there."[54] But
"as I understand *Brown*," he continued, "integration was not
to be accomplished through push button action but rather by
'deliberate speed.' " He was most concerned about considering
Cooper v. *Aaron* prematurely. "I know of no reason why we

should set aside all procedural rules in this case and still require other litigants to comply with the same," the justice wrote. "The case should be considered in its regular course, not by forced action. Of all tribunals this is one that should stick strictly to the rules. To do otherwise . . . [would] create the very situation that the Constitution prohibits, the existence of a preferred class." Clark did not pursue these sentiments, for he apparently never even had the rough drafts printed and circulated among his fellow justices for their consideration.[55]

Neither the calling of the special term nor a confrontation between Faubus and the Court was of primary concern to Justice Frankfurter. He believed that integration could be achieved in the South peacefully, if the Court cultivated southern moderates, particularly southern lawyers. To Frankfurter, Wayne Upton, president of the Little Rock school board, and the board's attorney, Richard C. Butler, exemplified such moderate sentiment. Frankfurter wrote to Justice Harlan that this sentiment "ought to be won, and I believe will be won, to the transcending issue of the Supreme Court as the authoritative organ of what the Constitution requires." In "everything we do, and how we do it," he said, "we must serve as exemplars of understanding and wisdom and magnanimity to the Butlers and Uptons of the South, as well as to the younger generation who not only recognize the inevitability of desegregation but want to further the acceptance of action of such inevitability."[56]

Frankfurter was committed enough to this idea that he urged Warren to begin the September 11 hearing of the case with a statement to Butler. Frankfurter wanted Warren to inform Butler that the Court took notice of the school board's defiance of Faubus as shown by its postponement of the beginning of school to September 15. The justice's rationale for such a move was, he wrote to Warren, "that the ultimate hope for the peaceful solution of the basic problem largely depends on winning the support of lawyers of the South for the overriding issue of obedience to the Court's decision. Therefore I think we should encourage every manifestation of fine conduct by a lawyer like Butler."[57]

COOPER v. *AARON* AND RENEWED
CONFRONTATION

Suspense mounted as the trial date approached. In Little Rock Governor Faubus waited to sign into law and act upon the recently passed segregation legislation.[58] School board members were resigned to defeat, but were not totally without hope that the Court might hold in their favor. Chief Justice Warren's unexpected announcement of the special term found attorney A. F. House on a trip to Europe, which meant that Richard Butler would argue the school board's case alone.[59] Chief counsel for Arkansas public utilities and various corporate firms, this World War II veteran was known for earnest, persuasive, and tightly reasoned trial arguments. Impressed with such qualities, one newspaperman described him as a lawyer of "judicial calm."[60] Thurgood Marshall and the NAACP were prepared to meet Butler's arguments with their fullest defense of the constitutional rights of Little Rock's black young people.[61] The media portrayed the case as the most significant test of integration since *Brown*.[62]

Immediately before the arguments were to begin on September 11 the Court held a thirty-minute private conference to discuss the proceedings. A majority voted against Frankfurter's idea of making a sympathetic opening statement to Butler. The refusal suggested how the Court had changed its perception of the central issues of the case. In the original trial before Judge Lemley, the issue had been whether a delay was justified in light of severe disruptions of the educational process. The central question in the court of appeals had become whether local resistance to integration, which was behind the disruption, was consistent with the standards established in *Brown II*. At the time the special term was called in August, the justices had had divergent views. But by the trial date—against the background of the actions of Faubus and the Arkansas legislature, the criticism by the state chief justices, and the media's efforts—the Court had come to see the case more or less in terms of state defiance of federal judicial authority. Given this perception, the issue perhaps seemed too great to permit the taking of Frankfurter's accommodationist approach.[63]

The Court's central concern in the case became apparent during the oral arguments.[64] Justice Brennan asked Butler whether the actions of Arkansas's governor and legislature violated the supremacy clause of the Constitution.[65] Warren was more direct. He asked the school board's attorney whether "the real issue before this Court is not just whether the School Board is frustrating the rights of these children, but whether the acts of any agency of the State of Arkansas are preventing them from exercising their constitutional rights?"[66] Clearly concerned by the measures proposed by Faubus and passed by the special session of the Arkansas legislature, the Court pressed Butler further to explain what the board planned to do during the postponement period it was seeking.[67] Privately, of course, Butler and the school board hoped that after two and a half years Faubus would be out of office. In response to the Court's questions, however, Butler suggested that the delay was needed simply "to let things . . . simmer down" and to test the segregation legislation in court.[68]

Firmly convinced of his assessment of southern moderate lawyers, Frankfurter attempted to draw from Butler responses that would suggest to the Court the wisdom of the position he had taken in conference. "Am I right to infer," the justice asked, "that you suggest that the mass of people in Arkansas are law-abiding, are not mobsters; they do not like desegregation, but they may be won to respect for the Constitution as pronounced by the organ charged with the duty of declaring it, and therefore adjusting themselves to it, although they may not like it?" The attorney warmly accepted Frankfurter's perspective, but the rest of the Court remained unconvinced.[69] The questions directed at the black children's counsel, Thurgood Marshall, were cast in terms of an overall concern for the federal court's ability to defend a minority's constitutional rights.[70]

Immediately following the oral arguments the Court met in private conference. After no more than thirty minutes, the justices decided to uphold the court of appeals' overruling of Judge Lemley's decision. Frankfurter and Harlan were selected to draft the order, which would be issued the following day. A full opinion, detailing the Court's reasons for its decision, would be handed down no later than October 6. Chief Justice Warren

chose Justice Brennan to write this opinion. On September 12
the Court issued a unanimous three-paragraph order charging
the school board with the duty to continue its plan of integration. In its order, the Court took notice of the fact that the Little
Rock schools were set to open on September 15. "In view of
the imminent commencement of the new school year at the
Central High School of Little Rock, Arkansas, we deem it important to make prompt announcement of our judgment af-
firming the Court of Appeals," wrote Justice Frankfurter. "The
expression of the views supporting our judgment will be prepared and announced in due course."[71]

Governor Faubus's response to the Court's order was one of
resistance. After a brief silence, he signed into law the legislation passed during the special legislative session of late August. Under one of these laws the governor called a special
election for September 27 to decide whether all of the city's public
high schools should open on an integrated basis—or close down.
He then announced that if voters rejected integrated education,
a recently chartered private school corporation would take over
the buildings of Little Rock's schools and operate them on a
segregated basis. To local voters, Faubus thus offered a means
of preserving segregation through taxpayers' support. Stressing the threat of outsiders, judicial dictatorship, Communism,
and federal authoritarianism, the governor issued an executive
order closing the schools until the referendum was held. He
grounded his order on an exercise of police powers, necessary
in order to prevent impending disorder, though no attempt was
made to show that any disorder was in fact imminent. Faubus
defended his action in terms of states' rights and democracy,
since the voters would decide whether to permanently close the
schools during the 1958–1959 academic year.[72]

But the Supreme Court's mandate of September 12 also generated other responses. Evidently the governor's willingness to
support the closing down of the public schools created confusion among some segregationists: two local segregationists filed
suit to prohibit the governor from interfering with the schools,
though nothing came of the suit. More importantly, the announced use of taxpayers' money to fund a private school corporation was rejected as unconstitutional in a newspaper ad-

vertisement signed by several prominent Little Rock attorneys. The most important reaction, however, was the formation of the Women's Emergency Committee to Open Our Schools (WEC), a small group of wives of prominent young businessmen and professional leaders who favored limited integration. Ever since the fall of 1957, Little Rock's business and professional elite, though generally moderate in its view of integration, had been divided and fragmented. The organization of the women's group, connected as it was with significant financial and social leadership, indicated that a few moderates were at last willing to challenge the governor and take a stand against segregation.[73]

As events unfolded in Little Rock, Justice Brennan worked over successive drafts of what would become the Court's formal opinion in the case of *Cooper* v. *Aaron*. Brennan began writing on September 17. For more than a week he wrote drafts and circulated them along his colleagues for comments. As this process continued, it was apparent that the justices wanted a firm, well-reasoned statement attesting to the Court's duty to uphold constitutional principle against local defiance. At one point Brennan included language urging congressional legislation to support desegregation. Suggesting that issues involving the Supreme Court's authority were of chief concern to a majority of the justices, Clark wrote forcefully, *"Leave out about Congress."*[74] As the drafting process continued it was apparent that Brennan and his brethren were influenced by the local situation in Little Rock.

On September 23 Governor Faubus requested the school board to surrender authority over Little Rock's schools. In accordance with provisions passed during the August legislative special session, Faubus asked the board to transfer administrative control to a newly chartered private school corporation. On the private suggestion of the Justice Department, however, public school officials refused the governor's request until they could obtain guidance from the federal district court.[75] Following this private advice, the school board petitioned the court "as to whether it would be in violation of that court's integration orders if it permitted a private school to be taught in the Central High School building during the period that the building is closed for public purposes, as authorized by Arkansas statutes, . . . such private school to be operated on a segregated basis." [76]

At this point the issue became even more clouded. After the Supreme Court had overturned his decision, Judge Lemley retired from the federal bench. Temporarily assigned to fill the opening was Judge John Miller who, of course, had heard the original Little Rock case in 1956. On September 23 Miller denied the school board's petition for instructions. The next day, NAACP lawyers challenged the constitutionality of the private school corporation. Making a significant departure from its established pattern of reluctance to initiate independent action, the Justice Department finally became an *amicus* party to the NAACP's suit. Judge Miller declined to prevent the transfer of public educational facilities to the private corporation because, he said, such action required consideration by a special three-judge tribunal. [77]

These and other developments influenced the Court's opinion process. On the morning of September 24, the *Washington Post* ran a banner headline: "Faubus Plan Put Up to Court." The Supreme Court met in conference to discuss Brennan's third draft that very morning, and, confronted with a continually shifting local situation, Justice Brennan and his colleagues worked to refine their position. On September 27 the people of Little Rock voted 19,470 to 7,561 to close the city's public high schools. [78] By September 29 the Court agreed on a final statement emphasizing that the case involved questions of the "highest importance to the maintenance of our federal system of government. It squarely presents a claim by the Governor and Legislature of a State that there is no duty on state officials to obey federal court orders resting on this Court's deliberate and considered interpretation of the United States Constitution." The opinion affirmed the consistency of this principle with the *Brown* decisions of 1954 and 1955; it further noted that in spite of several changes in the membership of the Court between 1954 and 1958, there had been no swerving among the justices from the principle established in *Brown*. Finally, the opinion also proclaimed that the private school corporation "cannot be squared with" the equal protection clause of the Fourteenth Amendment. [79] At noon on September 29 the Court convened for forty-five minutes to announce its opinion. [80]

Justice Frankfurter, after much disagreement with his colleagues, had some words to add in a concurring opinion released early in October. From his experience as a law professor at Harvard University, Justice Frankfurter had developed a certain sense of kinship with southern lawyers and legal academics. He maintained a regular correspondence with attorneys in the South, and no doubt considered these contacts a useful gauge of professional opinion.[81] He conceived of his concurring opinion (the overall argument of which differed little from that of the majority) as a sign of support for and encouragement to the southerners. "I myself am of the strong conviction," the justice later wrote to a friend concerning his concurrence, "that it is to the legal profession of the South on which our greatest reliance must be placed for a gradual thawing of the ice, not because they may not dislike termination of segregation but because . . . [they] will gradually realize that there is a transcending issue." This issue was, he concluded, "respect for law as determined so impressively by a unanimous Court in construing the Constitution of the United States."[82] Whether Justice Frankfurter in fact achieved his purpose remained unclear, but at least one southern lawyer responded with a letter advising him to resign.[83]

The Court's principal opinion in *Cooper* became law in Little Rock on September 29, but only nominally. On that date, after rather extraordinary procedures, a hastily called two-judge federal court of appeals meeting in Omaha relayed the decision to the city's federal district attorney.[84] On the same day the Little Rock school board signed an agreement leasing the public schools to the private school corporation. The court of appeals order implementing the Supreme Court's decision overruled this move, and on November 10 it directly ordered the school board to carry out its integration plan. But the schools remained closed.[85] The NAACP's suit challenging the private school corporation was in progress, but no decision was expected for months.[86] Reasoning that they had done all they could, for more than a year, to comply with the law, five of the six members of the school board and Superintendent Blossom resigned on November 12.[87]

Another factor to be considered was the surprise victory of Dale Alford over Brooks Hays in the race for Congress. Hays had served his congressional district for eight terms. He had attempted, unsuccessfully, to mediate between Faubus and Eisenhower early in the crisis. Alford, an eye specialist with strong segregationist convictions, was a member of the Little Rock school board. Two weeks before the November 4 congressional election he initiated a write-in campaign to get his name on the ballot. Insisting on the value of segregation and the threat of communism, Alford won. Hays's defeat indicated the level of pro-segregationist sentiment that had engulfed Little Rock.[88]

THE MODERATES REGAIN CONTROL

By mid-November it seemed that the Supreme Court had indeed "made nothing happen" to bring about desegregation.[89] Governor Faubus's clout in Little Rock and across the state seemed as strong as ever. The governor's supporters prepared new legislation which would make possible the packing of local school boards and the attainment of other segregationist goals; the measures would be introduced in the forthcoming regular February and March session of the Arkansas assembly.[90] Complicating matters further was the status of the school board. Following the resignation of the five members, only Alford technically retained a seat, but his congressional victory meant that he too must leave the board. Thus, in the heat of crisis, Little Rock's citizens would have to vote on filling the vacant positions.[91] In addition, NAACP efforts at getting *Cooper* enforced were stalled in Judge Miller's court, which contributed further to the stalemate.[92]

December 6 was the date set for school elections, and they became yet another contest over desegregation. Prior to the elections, the Little Rock Chamber of Commerce persuaded five prominent business and professional leaders to run. A significant factor influencing the Chamber's action was the pernicious impact the crisis had had on the city's business. The candidates did not publicly acknowledge the assistance of the Women's Emergency Committee, which had worked diligently against the school closing referendum; but privately the five moderates accepted the organization's aid and support. In line with the position of the Chamber of Commerce, the moderates campaigned on the need to open the schools on a basis consistent with the minimum plan of integration that had been affirmed by the federal courts. The segregationists also nominated a slate, but their position was weakened when a split developed among members of the Capital Citizens' Council, the most vocal segregationist group. This split resulted in the running of two rival sets of segregationist candidates, and as a consequence three moderates and three segregationists were elected.[93]

A new round of legal maneuvering began early in 1959. On January 6 Thurgood Marshall and Wiley Branton, along with the Justice Department, requested from Judge Miller an order that would desegregate the city's schools immediately. The judge refused, asking instead that the school board provide what amounted to a new desegregation plan. The board declined and requested that Miller permit it to open the schools on a segregated basis. The Justice Department responded by urging Miller to consider initiating contempt proceedings if the school board did not move to open desegregated high schools. The judge turned down the board's appeal; he also expressed disapproval of the department's request. The NAACP and the Justice Department did not appeal Miller's decision, but instead filed a new suit testing the constitutionality of the school closing laws. Marshall decided to file this new litigation rather than appeal the original case because, he told a department lawyer, "it was obvious" that Judge Miller would not hand down a favorable decision. A three-judge federal tribunal was mandated to hear the new case, but it could not convene until the spring.[94]

Meanwhile, the election of three moderates to the school board nudged Little Rock business leaders toward taking a firmer public stand on desegregation. In February 1959 officials of the Chamber of Commerce made a formal poll of its members by mail, asking for responses to two questions: (1) "Do you favor Little Rock's continuing with closed public schools?" and (2) "Do you now favor the reopening of Little Rock's public high schools on a controlled minimum plan of integration acceptable to the Federal Courts?" The responses to the first question were: yes, 230; no, 632; not voting, 285. The responses to the second question were: yes, 819; no, 245; not voting, 83. Encouraged, the board of directors of the Chamber issued a formal resolution on March 23 stating that it was a matter of practical necessity to follow the Supreme Court's decision in *Brown*. By implication, this view applied to *Cooper* v. *Aaron* as well.[95]

The resolution represented a concise statement of the legal justification for integration asserted by moderates since 1954: "The decision of the Supreme Court of the United States, however much we dislike it, is the declared law and is binding upon us. We think that the decision was erroneous and that it was a reversal of established law upon an unprecedented basis of psychology and sociology." However, the statement continued, "We must in honesty recognize that, because the Supreme Court is the Court of last resort in the country, what it has said must stand until there is a correcting constitutional amendment or until the Court corrects its own error."[96] The resolution also stressed two other principles. The Little Rock schools should be opened "using a pupil placement system acceptable to the school board and the Federal courts." As noted above, pupil placement laws gave school boards great discretion in the placement of students in local school districts so long as race was not the basis for transfers. The resolution also urged the school board to make sure that the contracts of "all teachers" would be "promptly renewed, in order that we do not lose our valuable and loyal staff."[97]

The latter statement was a response to rumors that segregationists sought to prevent the renewal of certain teachers' contracts. These rumors had been given credence by the introduction in the Arkansas legislature of bills to give the governor authority to appoint additional members to the Little Rock school board. On February 9, 1959, Governor Faubus had told newsmen that he favored not rehiring the principal and two vice principals at Central because of their actions during the crisis in the fall of 1957. The next day one of the segregationist members of the board, who claimed to speak for his two colleagues, said that some teachers should not be reemployed because of "their views on integration and segregation." The bill, as it turned out, was defeated by filibuster.[98]

Events now began moving toward a climax. In late March the Arkansas legislature passed a new set of segregationist bills concerning such matters as prohibitions on hiring NAACP members, tuition grants, and blood bank labels registering racial distinctions. By the spring of 1959 Governor Faubus's legal policies regarding integration were little different from those espoused by Jim Johnson and Amis Guthridge.[99] In late April and early May the Arkansas Supreme Court sanctioned two of the segregation measures. In one suit, taxpayers of the Little Rock school district challenged the use of public funds to support private schools;[100] in another, they questioned the constitutionality of the school closing act itself. The Arkansas supreme tribunal upheld lower court decisions that declared the two measures constitutional.[101] Only in regard to the school closing act was the majority's position questioned: in dissent, Justice E. F. McFaddin argued that "the Arkansas Legislature cannot, under the guise of police power, enact legislation contrary to the Arkansas Constitution."[102] On May 4 the segregationist provisions finally came to trial in the federal tribunal; after hearing arguments, a three-judge court announced that it would issue its decision in mid-June.[103] By this time Little Rock young people had not attended high school for nearly a whole academic year, and despite the continued support given Faubus, there were growing indications that many of the city's parents could no longer tolerate such a disruption.[104]

As local citizens waited for final action by the federal court, segregationists' demands for the removal of more than forty teachers became the focal point in the prolonged conflict. According to state law and the school board's administrative procedures, decisions on renewal of teachers' contracts were made in the spring. A vote against renewing a contract amounted to dismissal. The school board met on May 5, with a large number of observers present from moderate and segregationist groups. Contract renewal was not formally on the board's agenda, but it became at once the central point of discussion. The board was split three to three on a motion not to renew the contract of school superintendent Terrell Powell. After repeated votes on other reappointments, the board remained deadlocked. After various parliamentary maneuvers, the three moderates walked out.[105]

During the three weeks following the walkout, events in Little Rock moved swiftly. The departure of the moderates left the

2. "A Tennessee Newsman: Economic Aftermath," in Wilson Record and Jane Cassels Record, eds., *Little Rock, U.S.A.* (San Francisco, 1960), 283. *SSN*, Mar. 1958, 2.

3. *SSN*, Dec. 1957, 2; Jan. 1958, 8; Feb. 1958, 12. *Duncan* v. *Kirby*, 3 *RRLR* 434 (Ark. Sup. Ct. 1958); *Jackson et al.* v. *Kuhn*, ibid., 447 (U.S.C.A. 8th Cir. 1958); *Thomason* v. *Cooper*, ibid., 451 (U.S.C.A. 8th Cir. 1958).

4. *SSN*, Jan. 1958, 8.

5. Ibid., Dec. 1957, 2.

6. Ibid., Mar. 1958, 2; Apr. 1958, 12. Orval Eugene Faubus, *Down from the Hills* (Little Rock, 1980), 209, 307, 310–311.

7. 3 *RRLR* 1246 (1958).

8. John Thomas Elliff, "The United States Department of Justice and Individual Rights, 1937–1962" (Ph.D. diss., Harvard University, 1967), 603.

9. *SSN*, Dec. 1957, 2; Feb. 1958, 12; Mar. 1958, 2. See also *Jackson* v. *Kuhn*, 3 *RRLR* 447 (1958); and *Thomason* v. *Cooper*, 3 *RRLR* 451 (1958).

10. Osro Cobb, "*United States* v. *Governor Orval E. Faubus et Al.*" (manuscript, University of Arkansas at Little Rock, Archives, n.d.). *SSN* Mar. 1958, 2. Irving J. Spitzberg, Jr., "Racial Politics in Little Rock, 1954–1964" (manuscript, 1978), 56–57.

11. Leon B. Catlett to Virgil T. Blossom, Sept. 4, 1957; Catlett to Eugene C. Fisher, Dec. 6, 1957, LBCF.

12. A. F. House, interview with author, June 16, 1980. Richard C. Butler, interview with author, Jan. 28, 1980.

13. *SSN*, Dec. 1957, 2; Jan. 1958, 8. Cobb, "*U.S.* v. *Faubus.*"

14. Bates, *Long Shadow*, 63–116; Blossom, *It Has Happened Here*, 98–176.

15. Elliff, "Department of Justice," 602–603.

16. *SSN*, Feb. 1958, 12.

17. Ibid.

18. Elliff, "Department of Justice," 602–603.

19. *SSN*, Mar. 1958, 2, 3. See also *Cooper* v. *Aaron*, *Petition*, RCBF.

20. *SSN*, Mar. 1958, 2, 3. *Cooper* v. *Aaron*, *Petition*, RCBF. *Aaron* v. *Cooper*, "Petition by School Board," 3 *RRLR* 621 (1958).

21. Elliff, "Department of Justice," 603–604.

22. *SSN*, Mar. 1958, 2; Apr. 1958, 12. See also 3 *RRLR* 170 (1958). For discussion of Judge Davies's role see chap. 4.

23. *SSN*, Apr. 1958, 12. See also Faubus, *Down from the Hills*, 357–374.

24. See note 23 above. See also *U.S. News & World Report*, May 30, 1958.

25. *SSN*, May 1958, 6.

26. Ibid., June 1958, 11; Apr. 1958, 12. See also "The Story of Little Rock—As Governor Faubus Tells It," *U.S. News & World Report*, June 20, 1958, 101–106; Faubus, *Down from the Hills*, 357–374.

27. *Faubus v. U.S.*, 3 *RRLR* 439 (U.S.C.A. 8th Cir. 1958).

28. *Thomason v. Cooper*, 3 *RRLR* 451 (1958).

29. *Jackson v. Kuhn*, 3 *RRLR* 447 (1958). For more on cases cited in notes 28 and 29 see *SSN*, May 1958, 6.

30. *SSN*, June 1958, 10.

31. "Designation of District Judge to Handle Proceedings Not on His Docket," order from Archibald K. Gardner, C.J., U.S.C.A. for 8th Cir. to Federal District Judge Harry J. Lemley. Judge Harry J. Lemley Papers, Box 1, File 1 (UALR, Archives) (hereafter cited as JHJLP [UALR, A]). Judge Lemley's assignment was for the *Cooper* case for a period running from Apr. 21 to Sept. 1, 1958.

32. *Arkansas Democrat* Apr. 21, 1958. See also Elliff, "Department of Justice," 604.

33. *Arkansas Gazette*, June 22, 1958; "New Judge for CHS Has Roots in South," *Arkansas Democrat*, May 4, 1958.

34. Elliff, "Department of Justice," 604.

35. For briefs and court papers involving counsels' arguments see *Aaron v. Cooper*, *Petition*, RCBF, and those of NAACP LDF. For revised petition see 3 *RRLR* 624 (1958). For printed record see *Aaron v. Cooper*, 163 F. Supp. 13 (E.D. Ark.), *cert. denied*, 357 U.S. 566, *reversed en banc*, 257 F.2d ee (8th Cir.), *affirmed*, 358 U.S. 1 (1958). For the NAACP's side see Bates, *Long Shadow*, 151–55. For Judge Lemley's order for revision of petition see "Central High Delay Hangs on Two Points," *Arkansas Gazette*, June 8, 1958; and concerning Wayne Upton's comment see "Run of the News," *Arkansas Democrat*, June 13, 1958.

36. See *Arkansas Democrat*, June 13, 1958; and for media attention see scrapbook in JHJLP (UALR, A).

37. Elliff, "Department of Justice," 604.

38. 163 F. Supp. 13 (E.D. Ark. 1958).

39. *New York Times* June 22, 1958; *Arkansas Democrat*, June 22, 1958; *Newsweek*, June 30, 1958. See also Faubus, *Down from the Hills*, 380–382; J. W. Peltason, *Fifty-Eight Lonely Men: Southern Federal Judges and School Desegregation* (New York, 1961), 186.

40. *New York Times*, June 22, 1958; *Arkansas Democrat*, June 22, 1958; *Newsweek*, June 30, 1958. For process matters see the Supreme Court's order at 357 U.S. 567; Frankfurter, J., Draft Order (June 27, 1958), File [*Cooper*] (Aug. Spec. Term 1958), Felix Frankfurter Papers, (Manuscript Division, Harvard Law School) and (Library of Congress) (hereafter cited as FFP [HLS] and [LC]).

41. Elliff, "Department of Justice," 605–606. Here Elliff notes an error in Peltason's account in *Fifty-Eight Lonely Men*, 186.

42. Faubus, *Down from the Hills*, 375–396, 398.

43. *Cooper* v. *Aaron*, 358 U.S. 1, 13–14 (1958). Chief Judge Gardner expressed his regrets to Judge Lemley for the reversal Aug. 27, 1958, A–10, Box 2, File 4, JHJLP (UALR, A).

44. Elliff, "Department of Justice," 606.

45. For the deliberations between Justices Charles Evans Whittaker and William Joseph Brennan, Jr., see Justice Brennan, interview with author, Mar. 3, 1980. For process in general, see HHBP, Box 325, Legal (Aug. Special Term 1958), Case #1, Notes and Memos; Telegram, Aug. 26. Peltason, *Fifty-Eight Lonely Men*, 187. For the announcement concerning the procedure for hearing arguments for the special term, the formal filing of petitions, and the oral argument of Sept. 8, see *Cooper* v. *Aaron* 358 U.S. 1, 4, 14. The Justice Department was also under public pressure to act from U.S. Senator Jacob Javits.

46. "How U.S. Judges Feel about the Supreme Court," *U.S. News & World Report*, Oct. 24, 1958; Alexander M. Bickel, "An Inexplicable Document," *New Republic*, 139 (Sept. 1958), 9–11 (Morton J. Horwitz drew my attention to the latter reference). Walter F. Murphy, *Congress and the Court: A Case Study in the American Political Process* (Chicago, 1962), 224–225.

47. Faubus, *Down from the Hills*, 409–415; Peltason, *Fifty-Eight Lonely Men*, 189; DBP (SHSW, AD), and Bates, *Long Shadow*, 63–116; Press Release, Department of Justice (Sept. 9, 1958), Box 325, Harold J. Burton Papers (Library of Congress) (hereafter cited as HHBP [LC]); Dennis J. Hutchinson, "Unanimity and Desegregation: Decisionmaking in the Supreme Court, 1948–1958," *Georgetown Law Journal*, 68 (Oct. 1979), 76. The bills are reprinted in 3 *RRLR* 1048–1049 (1958).

48. *Cooper* v. *Aaron*, 358 U.S. 1, 4, 14 (1958).

49. Elliff, "Department of Justice," 607.

50. Ibid.

51. Ibid., 609.

52. Ibid.

53. Ibid., 609, 610.

54. File 1265, Box 65, FFP (LC), Clark, Draft Dissenting Opinion (no date), File 1 [*Cooper*] (Aug. Special Term 1958), Thomas C. Clark Papers (University of Texas), in Hutchinson, "Unanimity and Desegregation," 76.

55. Ibid.

56. Frankfurter to Warren (Sept. 11, 1958), File 1265, Box 65, FFP (LC).

57. Ibid.

58. Faubus, *Down from the Hills*, 409–415; Peltason, *Fifty-Eight Lonely Men*, 189; Bates, *Long Shadow*, 63–116.

59. House interview, June 16, 1980. Butler interview, Jan. 28, 1980.

60. House interview, June 16, 1980. Butler interview, Jan. 28, 1980.

61. Thurgood Marshall to Frank B. Robinson, Aug. 25, 1958, Drawer #33, "Mason" File, NAACP LDF.

62. *New York Times*, June 22, 1958; *Newsweek*, June 30, 1958.

63. Justice Harold H. Burton Diary (Sept. 11, 1958), Box 4, HHBP (LC).

64. Philip B. Kurland and Gerhard Casper, eds., *Landmark Briefs and Arguments of the Supreme Court of the United States: Constitutional Law* (Chicago, 1975), 54: 665–7301. Peltason, *Fifty-Eight Lonely Men*, 189–90. Stephen L. Wasby, Anthony A. D'Amato, and Rosemary Metrailer, *Desegregation from Brown to Alexander: An Exploration of Supreme Court Strategies* (Carbondale, 1977), 175–177.

65. Kurland and Casper, *Landmark Briefs*, 54: 685–686.

66. Ibid., 680–682, 687–688.

67. Ibid., 677–679, 695.

68. Ibid., 678. For the board's private reasons for requesting the delay, see Butler interview, Jan. 28, 1980.

69. Kurland and Casper, *Landmark Briefs*, 54: 703–704.

70. Ibid., 711–717, 722–727.

71. Burton Diary (Sept. 11 and 12, 1958). For the order of Sept. 12, see 358 U.S. 5.

72. Faubus, *Down from the Hills*, 425, 427, 440, 445. See also Peltason, *Fifty-Eight Lonely Men*, 195; and 3 *RRLR* 869 (1958).

73. Faubus, *Down from the Hills*, 430, 440. Henry M. Alexander, *The Little Rock Recall Election* (New York, 1960). Incisive examinations of the WEC and the response of the Little Rock business-professional elite in general may be found in Spitzberg, "Racial Politics," especially 28, 74; and Dr. Elizabeth Jacoway's essay on Little Rock in Jacoway and David R. Colburn, eds., *Southern Businessmen and Desegregation* (Baton Rouge, 1982).

74. For the drafts of the Supreme Court opinion see Brennan Draft Opinion (Sept. 17, 1958), Box 325, HHBP (LC) or File 1 [*Cooper*] (Aug. Special Term 1958). These and other drafts were discussed in Burton to Brennan (Sept. 18, 1958), Box 325 HHBP (LC); Harlan to Clark (Sept. 19, 1958), Box 325, HHBP (LC); Harlan to Brennan (Sept. 23, 1958), Box 325, HHBP (LC); 1958 Burton Diary (Sept. 19, 1958). See also Earl Warren, *The Memoirs of Earl Warren* (New York, 1977), 298.

75. Elliff, "Department of Justice," 610.

76. Ibid., 610–611.

77. Ibid., 611. See also material in RCBF cited in note 1 above. For

168 The Little Rock Crisis

the NAACP's and the school board's petition, see 3 *RRLR* 872, 875 (1958); for Miller's order see 3 *RRLR* 887.

78. The headline was in the *Washington Post*, Sept. 24, 1958, 1, col. 3; the Court's conference is referred to in 1958 Burton Diary (Sept. 24, 1958). For the local response and referendum, see Faubus, *Down from the Hills*, 442, 445; Alexander, *Recall Election*, 7–8. For the legal action, see 3 *RRLR* 872, 883, 885; *Aaron* v. *Cooper*, 261 F.2d 97 (8th Cir. 1958) (per curiam), on remand, 169 F. Supp. 325 (E.D. Ark. 1959). The closing and leasing laws were ultimately found unconstitutional in *Aaron* v. *McKinley*, 173 F. Supp. 944 (E.D. Ark.) (Per curiam affirmed per curiam sub nom.); *Faubus* v. *Aaron*, 361 U.S. 197 (1959).

79. Brennan Draft Opinion (Sept. 25, 1958), Box 325, HHBP (LC).

80. *Cooper* v. *Aaron*, 3 *RRLR* 855 (1958). See Hutchinson, "Unanimity and Desegregation," 73–86, an excellent expository discussion of the decisional process. 1958 Burton Diary (Sept. 29, 1958) discusses the conference. Peltason, *Fifty-Eight Lonely Men*, 190–191, and Wasby et al., *Desegregation*, 177–179, discuss the announcement of the opinion.

81. Hutchinson, "Unanimity and Desegregation," 83–85. See also Monte M. Lemann to Frankfurter, Nov. 6, 1958, Box 107, F. 8, FFP (HLS). See House interview, June 16, 1980, and Butler interview, Jan. 28, 1980, for comments concerning Justice Frankfurter's correspondence with Harvard Law School graduates in Little Rock. Professor Robert Leflar of the University of Arkansas School of Law, also a Harvard Law graduate, reiterated this point. Professor Leflar also pointed out the debt Frankfurter felt to former U.S. senator and former American Bar Association president U. M. Rose of Arkansas for early involvement in the ABA after the former's graduation from law school. Other correspondence in the Frankfurter Papers both at Harvard Law School and the Library of Congress confirms that the Arkansas contacts were part of a larger network throughout the South.

82. Frankfurter, J., to C. C. Burlingham, Nov. 12, 1958, File 644, Box 37, FFP (LC). For further references see Hutchinson, "Unanimity and Desegregation," 84 n. 710.

83. William F. Daniel to Frankfurter, Oct. 7, 1958, Box 107 F. 8., FFP (HLS). For media comments see Hutchinson, "Unanimity and Desegregation," 84, nn. 711–714. Drafts of the concurrence itself are in FFP (HLS). For official record see 3 *RRLR* 862 (1958).

84. 3 *RRLR* 893 (1958). Wiley Branton interview with author, Dec. 11, 1979, also provided insight into the complex procedural issues. Hutchinson, "Unanimity and Desegregation," 73–86.

85. Peltason, *Fifty-Eight Lonely Men*, 198; *Aaron* v. *Cooper*, 261 F.2d 97 (8th Cir. 1958) (per curiam), on remand, 169 F. Supp. 325 (E.D. Ark. 1959). See also "School Board Resolution Authorizing Lease," 3 *RRLR* 887, 893, 894 (1958).

86. *Aaron et al.* v. *Ed. I. McKinley*, 4 *RRLR* 543 (U.S.D.C. E.D. Ark. 1959).

87. Alexander, *Recall Election*, 6–8; Faubus, *Down from the Hills*, 474–478.

88. Alexander, *Recall Election*, 6–8; Faubus, *Down from the Hills*, 474–478. See also Brooks Hays, *Politics Is My Parish* (Baton Rouge, 1981), 197–208.

89. The comment refers to an assessment of *Brown* in Alexander M. Bickel, *The Least Dangerous Branch: The Supreme Court at the Bar of Politics* (Indianapolis, 1962), 245. Hutchinson, "Unanimity and Desegregation," 85, extends Bickel's assessment to the impact of *Cooper* v. *Aaron*.

90. Spitzberg, "Racial Politics," 95. The legislation (discussed below) when passed appeared in and was analyzed at 4 *RRLR* 390, 460, 747, 752–753, 765–767, 769, 770–771, 773, 775 (1959). See also Cobb, "*U.S.* v. *Faubus.*"

91. Alexander, *Recall Election*, 8–9.

92. Elliff, "Department of Justice," 612.

93. Alexander, *Recall Election*, 8–9; Spitzberg, "Racial Politics." Jacoway and Colburn, *Southern Businessmen*, 15–41. "Little Rock, Arkansas, School Desegregation," William F. Rogers Papers, Dwight D. Eisenhower Library Staff Files, Abilene, Kansas.

94. See Elliff, "Department of Justice," 612, for Marshall's quote and general discussion. For a summary of the newly filed case see *Aaron et al.* v. *Ed. I. McKinley*, 4 *RRLR* 543 (1959).

95. Alexander, *Recall Election*, 9. The Chamber of Commerce first publicly urged the federal court to open the schools on a segregated basis. This effort was futile. Spitzberg, "Racial Politics," 94.

96. Alexander, *Recall Election*, 10.

97. Ibid. On the pupil placement laws, see Wasby et al., *Desegregation*, 376–425; Frank T. Read and Lucy S. McGough, *Let Them Be Judged: The Judicial Integration of the Deep South* (Metuchen, N.J., 1978), 438; and chap. 3, 80.

98. Alexander, *Recall Election*, 10, 11. On the filibustered legislation see Spitzberg "Racial Politics," 95. The sponsor of the defeated measures was a "Faubus protégé."

99. See Governor Faubus's address, Jan. 13, 1959, 4 *RRLR* 179 (1959); see also 4 *RRLR* 390, 460, 747, 752–53, 769, 770–771, 773, 775 (1959) for text of legislation. Chaps. 3 and 4 discuss the Governor's accommodationist stragegy. Compare the approach discussed there with the analysis here.

100. *Fitzhugh et al.* v. *Ford*, 4 *RRLR* 550 (Ark. Sup. Ct. 1959).

101. *Garrett* v. *Faubus*, 4 *RRLR* 553 (Ark. Sup. Ct. 1959).

102. Ibid., 573.

103. *Aaron et al.* v. *Ed. I. McKinley*, 4 *RRLR* 543 (U.S.D.C. E.D. Ark. 1959).

104. Alexander, *Recall Election*, 11–12.

105. Ibid.

106. Ibid., 8–32.

107. Ibid.

108. *Aaron et al.* v. *Ed. I. McKinley*, 4 *RRLR* 543.

109. Elliff, "Department of Justice," 613.

110. "Little Rock, Arkansas, School Desegregation, William F. Rogers Papers.

111. Ibid.

A Summing Up _____

Long after the end of crisis in 1959, Little Rock retained a place in the nation's collective memory. In U.S. history textbooks new generations read about the conflict that led to military occupation of an American high school. As late as 1976, in connection with the media's reporting of the celebration of the Bicentennial of Independence in the states, a story on Arkansas began with film clips of the Central High disorders of September 23 and 24, 1957. By the 1980s, the struggle for equal justice had resulted in more tragic confrontations than that which had rocked the Arkansas capital. But from 1959 on Little Rock stood as a symbol of what was to come, not only in places like Selma, Alabama, but in Watts, Boston, Detroit, and elsewhere. Because Little Rock has become a symbol of a national travail, then, it demands renewed pondering and evaluation, not only to measure the degree of change, but to show what remains undone.

There were implications in the Little Rock story for future efforts to implement school desegregation in the narrow sense. The crisis and its origins revealed the extent to which desegregation sparked political dynamics that only indirectly involved race. Questions of local control, economic development, community values, individual rights, government authority, and representative democracy shaped, and were shaped by, the law's demand for equal educational opportunity. Yet the political pressures raised by these questions often proved too powerful for local or national leaders. Both Governor Faubus and President Eisenhower were unwilling to subordinate narrow electoral goals to the enforcement of moral principle. Even though the motives behind this unwillingness may not necessarily have been opportunistic, they nonetheless entangled desegregation in a morass of political considerations that invited confrontation. As the years went by southern leaders and the federal government became more adept at maneuvering in this morass. In Mississippi in the early 1960s, Governor Ross Barnett and U.S. Attorney General Robert F. Kennedy agreed in effect to a bogus conflict in which the governor would save face by resisting and then yielding by prearrangement to superior force.[1] There were of course variations but, after Little Rock, desegregation across America became an extension of politics by other means.

The politicization of desegregation in Little Rock had further ramifications for the grand effort to establish racial justice in America. After the Supreme Court's *Brown* decision in 1954, Little Rock officials, Arkansas state authorities, and the federal government itself approached racial justice not as a moral imperative but in terms of deference to constitutional symbolism and the rule of law. The focus on legalism, which continued at least until the 1980s, had the effect of confusing means with ends. Obedience to law itself—not the substantive value of equal educational opportunity—became the basis for both compliance and resistance. In short, many government leaders expected first southerners, then all Americans, to accept minority rights as a matter of compulsion rather than consent. Such an expectation demanded elected officials a level of wisdom in creating citizen support that was high indeed. Little Rock was a forewarning that such wisdom would be rare and that its absence would generate frustrations which in turn would lead to resorts to force—whether in the form of paratroopers, civil disobedience, race riots, busing, or affirmative action. Even though the use of force might seem understandable in some instances, in the long run dependence on it obscured the moral principle at issue.

Still another lesson of Little Rock concerned the relationship between the rule of law and judicial activism. Prior to and during the crisis of 1957–1959, the school board, white moderates, segregationists, the federal government, and Governor Faubus—virtually everyone including the NAACP and its black constituents—publicly based their response to *Brown* totally or in part on the idea of a government of law, not men. In *Cooper* v. *Aaron* the Supreme Court's broadly phrased assertion of its constitutional role emphasized the same principle. But focus on the rule-of-law value led inevitably to controversy over the nature of judicial power in a representative democracy. Segregationists, moderates, and integrationists represented a continuum of opinion ranging from vigorous condemnation of all but the barest minimum of judicial authority to the whole-hearted endorsement of broad-gauged judicial policy making. Underlying these opinions were assumptions about whether elected officials or the courts were the best means of maintaining the supremacy of law and the Constitution.

Nationally, this debate resulted in two theories of judicial power. One theory stressed the need for self-restraint in deciding cases, especially deferring to the legislative branch. Justice Felix Frankfurter was a leading spokesman for this position, and by the 1970s there were many who agreed with him. To the proponents of judicial self-restraint, permitting legislatures a primary role in lawmaking maintained values of local diversity and limited federal power that were vital to the preservation of the American constitutional order. Alexander Bickel, a Frankfurter protégé and influential legal academic, made this point in 1970. "It is diversity that the law will have to recognize as the essential value during the last third of the twentieth century," he said. "A striving for diversity is not necessarily in express conflict with the goal of an egalitarian society, but it connotes a different order of priorities."[2]

The second theory, of course, was judicial activism. Proponents of this view emphasized that in such vital areas of law as race relations, the majority's elected representatives had been chiefly responsible for limiting minority rights, democratic participation, and economic opportunity. To those holding these convictions, judicial limitation of legislative power would bring about justice. "For them," wrote leading activist and federal judge Skelly Wright, "there was no theoretical gulf between the law and morality; and, for them the [U.S. Supreme] Court was

the one institution in society that seemed to be speaking most
consistently the language of idealism which we all recited in
grade school. . . . They have seen that affairs can be ordered
in conformance to constitutional ideals and that injustice . . .
can be routed."³ While not denying the importance of local
community values, judicial activists gave greater priority to
sustaining individual liberty and equal justice.

What did Little Rock's experience suggest about the relative
impact of judicial activism and self-restraint? The community's
response to *Brown I* and *II* and the *Aaron* litigation from 1954 to
1959 demonstrated that judicial lawmaking could foster public
acceptance of desegregation. Acceptance occurred, however, only
after the judicial and democratic process enforced certain values over others. And before these values could be enforced the
relationships among popular consent, the rule of law, and constitutional principle had to be worked out in public events and
private negotiations. It was the interaction between legal process and political interest that gave force and meaning to values. But the chief result of this interaction was that questions
of moral principle became absorbed in a confrontation over the
scope, character, and legitimacy of federal authority. This process in turn narrowed the reach of the constitutional principle
established in *Brown* and reaffirmed in *Cooper* v. *Aaron*. Neither
opponents nor defenders of desegregation fully attained their
goals. Instead, the complex interplay of interests, democracy,
law, and values produced a policy of principled but conservative moderation.

Individual and community conduct changed, then, because
of judicial activism *and* democratic processes. But the changes
were limited and occurred only after conflict. Segregationists did
resort to violence; and their public pronouncements were certainly angry and full of hate. On the whole, however, they relied upon quixotic states' rights arguments to achieve victory
through elections and the courts. The NAACP depended upon
the federal courts to protect the constitutional rights of blacks;
but after their demand for a progressive integration program was
defeated at an early phase in the *Aaron* litigation they were reduced to defending the token, gradualist Blossom Plan. After
early rejection of a fairly progressive desegregation program, the

school board gave in to political pressures and repeatedly altered its plan. Changes were always in the direction of less and slower—that is, increasingly moderate—desegregation, but the board never denied an ultimate duty to comply with *Brown*. When the federal government and the Supreme Court became involved in Little Rock their role essentially concerned not whether a more progressive desegregation program might be implemented, but whether the school board's limited plan would become operative at all. Governor Faubus slowly but steadily embraced the segregationists' states' rights arguments; however, each time these were overturned, he (like the segregationists themselves) acquiesced to federal authority. Struggle over the enforcement of *Brown*'s moral and constitutional principle thus was channeled into legal and democratic processes, which brought about a triumph of moderation.

Contributing to this triumph were events unknown to the public. Repeatedly from 1957 to 1959 segregationists, the school board, Faubus, and the federal government entered into secret negotiations among themselves. The Justice Department also on occasion dealt privately with the NAACP. Private exchanges complicated the political situation, forcing even greater dependence on resolution through the courts and popular elections. The ultimate impact of this resolution was, nonetheless, the integration of a mere handful of black young people into Little Rock's two predominantly white high schools.

This was the immediate impact of judicial activism in Little Rock. From the 1960s on, the course of desegregation in that city and in the nation as a whole took many twists and turns. By 1981 Central High was a model of integration, and its honor-roll black student body president was on the way to becoming a freshman at Yale University. In the city's lower grades, however, blacks probably constituted a majority. In Boston, New York, Detroit, Chicago, St. Louis, Denver, Los Angeles, and other communities the imbalance was often far greater. Throughout the South, where progress was most noticeable, the difference between Little Rock's experience and that of New Orleans, where the public schools were less than 15 percent white, demonstrated the degree to which most students (white and black) attended racially imbalanced schools. Thus judicial activism had neither fulfilled the ideals of Judge Skelly Wright nor totally disrupted local community values, as feared by Frankfurter and Bickel. Instead, the changes in attitude wrought by *Brown* were significant, but essentially conservative. As for the intrinsic worth of racial justice as a moral principle, it was obscured in controversy over legalism and administrative forms.

In 1955, in the wake of the Supreme Court's *Brown II* opinion, one of America's foremost students of race relations made a prediction. He compared the ultimate failure of the First Reconstruction of the Civil War era with the potential for success of the Second Reconstruction that was then just under way. "However deliberate and halting its speed," he concluded, "the Second Reconstruction would seem to promise more enduring results."[4] From the perspective of nearly thirty years, the prophetic accuracy of this conclusion remains in doubt. What has become apparent, however, as another assessment of *Brown* has noted, is that "law in a democracy must contend with reality. It has to persuade. It has to induce compliance by its appeal to shared human values and social goals."[5] In Little Rock the courts and the democratic process achieved a degree of desegregation in which moderate conservatism triumphed over moral principle. This triumph virtually insured that a more meaningful fulfillment of the nation's democratic and constitutional ideals would demand greater commitment and striving. Here was the enduring lesson of Little Rock, a lesson the nation has not yet fully grasped.

NOTES

1. John Thomas Elliff, "The United States Department of Justice and Individual Rights, 1937–1962" (Ph.D. diss., Harvard University, 1967), 693–710.

2. Alexander Bickel, *The Supreme Court and the Idea of Progress* (New York, 1970), 112–113.

3. J. Skelly Wright, "Professor Bickel, the Scholarly Tradition, and the Supreme Court," *Harvard Law Review*, 84 (Feb. 1971), 804–805.

4. C. Vann Woodward, *The Strange Career of Jim Crow* (New York, 1957), 179.

5. Richard Kluger, *Simple Justice: The History of Brown v. Board of Education and Black America's Struggle for Equality* (1976; reprint, New York: Vintage Books, 1977), 742.

Bibliography ─────────

BOOKS

Alexander, Henry M., *The Little Rock Recall Election* (New York, 1960).

Arkansas Gazette, Crisis in the South: The Little Rock Story (Little Rock, 1958).

Bartley, Numan V., *The Rise of Massive Resistance: Race and Politics in the South during the 1950s* (Baton Rouge, 1969).

Bates, Daisy, *The Long Shadow of Little Rock, A Memoir* (New York, 1962).

Blossom, Virgil T., *It Has Happened Here* (New York, 1959).

Brown, Robert R., *Bigger Than Little Rock* (Greenwich, Conn., 1958).

Calhoun, John C., "Disquisition on Government," in *Works of John C. Calhoun*, 4 vols. (New York, 1863).

Campbell, Ernest Q., and Thomas F. Pettigrew *Christians in Racial Crisis: A Study of Little Rock's Ministry* (Washington, D.C., 1959).

Dabney, Virginius, *Across the Years: Memories of a Virginian* (Garden City, N.Y., 1978), 232–233.

Du Bois, W.E.B., *The Souls of Black Folk* (New York, 1903).

Faubus, Orval Eugene, *Down from the Hills* (Little Rock, 1980).

Fetner, Gerald L., *Ordered Liberty: Legal Reform in the Twentieth Century* (New York, 1983).

Foster, G. W., Jr., "Turning Point for Desegregation." In *American Education Today*, edited by Paul Woodring and John Scanlon (New York, 1963), 126–138.

Hays, Brooks, *Politics Is My Parish, An Autobiography* (Baton Rouge, 1981).

Hays, Brooks, *A Southern Moderate Speaks* (Chapel Hill, 1959).

Huckaby, Elizabeth, *Crisis at Central High, Little Rock, 1957–58* (Baton Rouge, 1980).

178   Bibliography

Jacoway, Elizabeth, and David R. Colburn, eds., *Southern Businessmen and Desegregation* (Baton Rouge, 1982).
Keys, V. O., Jr., *Southern Politics* (New York, 1949).
Kluger, Richard, *Simple Justice: The History of Brown v. Board of Education and Black America's Struggle for Equality* (1976; reprint New York, 1977).
Kurland, Philip B. and Gerhard Casper, eds., *Landmark Briefs and Arguments of the Supreme Court of the United States: Constitutional Law* (Chicago, 1975).
Lester, Jim, *A Man for Arkansas: Sid McMath and the Southern Reform Tradition* (Little Rock, 1976).
McMillen, Neil R., *The Citizens' Council: Organized Resistance to the Second Reconstruction, 1955–1964* (Urbana, Ill., 1971).
Murphy, Walter F., *Congress and the Court: A Case Study in the American Political Process* (Chicago, 1962).
Peltason, J. W., *Fifty-Eight Lonely Men: Southern Federal Judges and School Desegregation* (New York, 1961).
Read, Frank T., and Lucy S. McGough, *Let Them Be Judged: The Judicial Integration of the Deep South* (Metuchen, N.J., 1978).
Record, Wilson, and Jane Cassels Record, eds., *Little Rock, U.S.A.* (San Francisco, 1960).
Shannon, Karr, *Integration Decision Is Unconstitutional* (Little Rock, 1958).
Warren, Earl, *The Memoirs of Earl Warren* (New York, 1977).
Woodward, C. Vann, *The Strange Career of Jim Crow* (New York, 1957).
Wyatt-Brown, Bertram, *Southern Honor: Ethics and Behavior in the Old South* (New York, 1982).

NEWSPAPERS AND PERIODICALS

The Americana Annual (1956).
Arkansas Democrat (Little Rock).
Arkansas Gazette (Little Rock).
Bartley, Numan V., "Looking Back at Little Rock," *Arkansas Historical Quarterly*, 25 (Summer 1966), 101–116.
Bell, Derrick A., "Civil Rights Lawyers on the Bench," *Yale Law Journal*, 91 (March 1982), 826–836.
Bickel, Alexander M., "An Inexplicable Document," *New Republic*, 139 (September 1958), 27–28.
Clark, Thomas D., "Economic Basis of Southern Politics," *Forum*, 112 (August 1949), 8–16.
Freyer, Tony A., "Politics and Law in the Little Rock Crisis, 1954–1957," *Arkansas Historical Quarterly*, 40 (Autumn 1981), 195–219.

"How U.S. Judges Feel about the Supreme Court," *U.S. News & World Report*, October 24, 1958, 41.

Hutchinson, Dennis J., "Unanimity and Desegregation: Decisionmaking in the Supreme Court, 1948–1958," *Georgetown Law Journal*, 68 (October 1979), 1–96.

"Interposition vs. Judicial Power: A Study of Ultimate Authority in Constitutional Questions," 1 *Race Relations Law Reporter* (December 1956), 465.

"A Look at Dean Branton," *Barrister*, 8 (November 1979), 8–9.

"Military Powers of the Executive as Related to the Courts," 2 *Race Relations Law Reporter* 1071 (1957).

New York Times.

Race Relations Law Reporter.

Southern School News.

Stephan, A. Stephen, and Charles A. Hicks, "Integration and Segregation in Arkansas—One Year Afterward," *Journal of Negro Education*, 24 (1955), 170–185.

"The Story of Little Rock—As Governor Faubus Tells It," *U.S. News & World Report*, June 20, 1958, 15.

Wright, J. Skelly, "Professor Bickel, the Scholarly Tradition, and the Supreme Court," *Harvard Law Review*, 84 (February 1971), 84.

MISCELLANEOUS DOCUMENTS

Civil Rights Hearings before Subcommittee No. 5 of the Committee on the Judiciary, House of Representatives, Eighty-Fifth Congress, First Session (Washington, D.C., 1957).

Cobb, Osro, "United States v. Governor Orval E. Faubus et Al." (manuscript, University of Arkansas at Little Rock, Archives, n.d.).

Drummond, Boyce Alexander, Jr., "Arkansas Politics: A Study of a One-Party System" (Ph.D. diss., University of Chicago, 1957).

Elliff, John Thomas, "The United States Department of Justice and Individual Rights, 1937–1962" (Ph.D. diss., Harvard University, 1967).

Foster, G. W., Jr., "Brief Comparison of Function and Relationship between NAACP and the Legal Defense and Education Fund of the NAACP, Late 1950s" (memo to Tony Freyer, July 17, 1981).

Foster, G. W., Jr., "Education and Law: Segregation in Public Schools" (manuscript, Madison, Wis., 1962).

Spitzberg, Irving J., Jr., "Racial Politics in Little Rock, 1954–1964" (manuscript in Dr. Spitzberg's possession, 1978).

Tushnet, Mark, "Organizational Politics and Public Interest Law: Two Examples from the NAACP" (paper in Dr. Tushnet's possession, 1981).
Tushnet, Mark, "The NAACP White Primary Struggle in Mid-1940s" (memo to Tony Freyer, July 19, 1981).

MANUSCRIPTS

Aaron v. Cooper, Petition for Writ of Certiorari to the United States Court of Appeals for the Eighth Circuit, in the Supreme Court of the United States, October Term, 1958.
Aaron v. Cooper Files, NAACP Legal Defense and Education Fund Inc. (10 Columbus Circle, New York).
Daisy Bates Papers (State Historical Society of Wisconsin, Archives Division).
Harold H. Burton Papers (Library of Congress).
Richard C. Butler Case Files, *Cooper v. Aaron* (in Mr. Butler's possession, Little Rock).
Arthur B. Caldwell Papers (University of Arkansas, Fayetteville).
Leon B. Catlett Case File, *Aaron v. Cooper* (in Tony Freyer's possession).
Federal Bureau of Investigation Report—Little Rock, 44-12284-933 (FBI, Washington, D.C., and University of Arkansas at Little Rock).
Federal Bureau of Investigation Report—Little Rock, 44-12284-937 (FBI, Washington, D.C.).
Federal Bureau of Investigation Report—Little Rock, 44-12285-855 (FBI, Washington, D.C.).
Felix Frankfurter Papers (Manuscript Division, Harvard Law School).
Felix Frankfurter Papers (Library of Congress).
James C. Hagerty Papers (Dwight D. Eisenhower Library, Abilene, Kans.).
Georg G. Iggers Papers (University of Arkansas at Little Rock, Archives).
Harry J. Lemley Papers (University of Arkansas at Little Rock, Archives).
Mason File, NAACP Legal Defense and Education Fund, Inc. (10 Columbus Circle, New York).
National Association for the Advancement of Colored People, Group III, General Office File—Arkansas (Library of Congress).
William F. Rogers Papers (Dwight D. Eisenhower Library, Abilene, Kans.).
Schools: General File, NAACP Legal Defense Fund, Inc. (10 Columbus Circle, New York).

INTERVIEWS

Interviews with Author

Harry Ashmore, Santa Barbara, June 2, 1981.
Wiley Branton, Washington, D.C., December 11, 1979.
William J. Brennan, Jr., Washington, D.C., March 3, 1980.
Richard C. Butler, Little Rock, February 5, 1980.
Leon B. Catlett, Little Rock, July 1, 1980.
Ronald N. Davies, Washington, D.C., April 16, 1980.
Orval E. Faubus, Little Rock, July 15, 1980.
James Johnson, Little Rock, September 4, 1980.
A. F. House, Little Rock, June 16, 1980.
J. L. (Bex) Shaver, Wynne, Ark., August 15, 1980.
W. J. Smith, Little Rock, September 3, 1980.
Henry E. Spitzberg, Little Rock, September 25, 1980.
Ozell Sutton, Atlanta, November 14, 1980.

Dwight D. Eisenhower Administration Oral History Project (Columbia University):

Wiley Branton (1973)
William G. Cooper (1971)
Harold Engstrom (1971)
Amis Guthridge (1972)
A. F. House (1973)

CASES

Federal

Aaron v. *Cooper*, 1 *Race Relations Law Reporter* 851 (U.S.D.C. E.D. Ark. 1956).
Aaron v. *Cooper*, 2 *Race Relations Law Reporter* 593 (U.S.C.A. 8th Cir. 1957).
Aaron et al. v. *Ed. I. McKinley*, 4 *Race Relations Law Reporter* 543 (U.S.D.C. E.D. Ark. 1959).
Bolling v. *Sharpe*, 347 U.S. 497 (1954).
Brewer v. *Hoxie*, 1 *Race Relations Law Reporter* 1027 (U.S.C.A. 8th Cir. 1956).
Brown v. *Board of Education of Topeka, Kansas* (*Brown I*), 347 U.S. 483 (1954).

Brown v. *Board of Education* (*Brown II*), 349 U.S. 294 (1955).

Cooper v. *Aaron*, 358 U.S. 1 (1958).

Faubus v. *Aaron*, 361 U.S. 197 (1959).

Faubus v. *U.S.*, 3 *Race Relations Law Reporter* 439 (U.S.C.A. 8th Cir. 1958).

Fisher v. *Hurst*, 333 U.S. 147 (1948).

Henderson v. *U.S.*, 339 U.S. 816 (1950).

Hoxie v. *Brewer*, 1 *Race Relations Law Reporter* 43 (U.S.D.C. E.D. Ark. 1955).

Hoxie v. *Brewer*, 1 *Race Relations Law Reporter* 299 (U.S.D.C. E.D. Ark. 1956).

Jackson et al. v. *Kuhn*, 3 *Race Relations Law Reporter* 447 (U.S.C.A. 8th Cir. 1958).

Johnson v. *Crawfis* 1 *Race Relations Law Reporter* 151 (U.S.D.C. E.D. Ark. 1955).

McLaurin v. *Oklahoma State Regents*, 339 U.S. 637 (1950).

Missouri ex. rel. Gaines v. *Canada*, 305 U.S. 337 (1938).

Moyer v. *Peabody*, 212 U.S. 78 (1909).

Plessy v. *Ferguson*, 163 U.S. 537 (1896).

Sipuel v. *Board of Regents*, 332 U.S. 631 (1948).

Sterling v. *Constantin*, 287 U.S. 378 (1932).

Strutwear Knitting Co. v. *Olson*, 13 F. Supp. 384 (D.C. Minn. 1936).

Sweatt v. *Painter*, 339 U.S. 629 (1950).

Thomason v. *Cooper*, 3 *Race Relations Law Reporter* 451 (U.S.C.A. 8th Cir. 1958).

State

Duncan v. *Kirby*, 3 *Race Relations Law Reporter* 434 (Ark. Sup. Ct. 1958).

Garrett v. *Faubus*, 4 *Race Relations Law Reporter* 553 (Ark. Sup. Ct. 1959).

Index _____

184   Index

Burton, Justice Harold, 148
business boosterism, 11. *See also*
   business elite
business elite, 16-24, 29-30, 33,
   58-59, 94, 108, 139-163. *See also*
   Blossom Plan; *Cooper* v. *Aaron;*
   Women's Emergency Committee
Butler, Richard C., 46, 141, 145,
   151, 152-154

Caldwell, Arthur B., 95-104, 120,
   125, 149
Capital Citizens' Council, 24-25,
   32-33, 95, 100, 102, 120. *See*
   also Guthridge, Amis; interposition; segregationists; states'
   rights
Catlett, Leon B., 46, 52-59, 88,
   141
Central High School, 15-24, 28,
   44, 87, 92, 102-104, 116, 127,
   139, 163, 171, 175. *See also*
   Blossom Plan
Cherry, Francis, 23, 68, 74, 77,
   90
Chowning, Frank E., 46
Civil Rights Act of 1957, 97
Clark, Justice Tom C., 150-151,
   155
class relations, 17-18, 20-35, 45,
   94, 125, 162, 163. *See also Aaron*
   v. *Cooper*; Blossom Plan; business elite; segregationists
Clinton, Tennessee, 120
Cooper, William G., 41-42, 45,
   150
Cooper v. *Aaron*, 143-163, 173-174
Crenchaw, Rev. J. C., 26-27, 44,
   51-59, 129-130
CROSS campaign, 162

Davies, Judge Ronald N., 102,
   104-109, 118-126, 140

Deer, Rev. Lewis, 28
Du Bois, W.E.B., 3
Dunbar Jr. High School, 16-18,
   28. *See also* Blossom Plan

East Arkansas, 21-22, 33-35, 63,
   76-78, 81, 91, 96, 98. *See also*
   Faubus, Orval E.; interposition; states' rights
Eastland, James, 68
Eckford, Elizabeth, 104
Eisenhower, Dwight D., 10, 75,
   98, 105-109, 118-125, 127, 139-
   163, 172. *See also* U.S. Department of Justice
Engstrom, Harold J., 100

Faubus, Orval E., 23-24, 65, 73-
   82, 86-109, 115-119, 122-125,
   139-163, 172-175
Folkways, 31
Frankfurter, Justice Felix, 5-10,
   148-158, 173, 176

Gardner, Judge Archibald K., 55,
   145, 147
Griffin, Marvin, 100-101, 103, 133
Guthridge, Amis, 24-25, 65, 67,
   70, 91, 93-104, 118, 125, 142,
   144, 147, 161
Guy, Walter C., 140, 143

Haley, John, 145
Hall High School, 16-18, 45, 94,
   163
Harlan, Justice John Marshall, 8,
   153
Harper, Judge Ray W., 130
Hays, Brooks, 21, 106, 119, 123,
   124, 144, 147, 157-158
Henley, J. Smith, 143
Hoover, J. Edgar, 127
Horace Mann High School, 16-
   18, 42-45

186

Index

About the Author

TONY FREYER is Associate Professor of History and Law at the University of Alabama. He is the author of *Harmony and Dissonance: The Swift and Erie Cases in American Federalism* and *Forums of Order: The Federal Courts and Business in American History*. His articles have appeared in *Encyclopedia of American Political History*, *Business History Review*, *Law and Southern History*, *The Wisconsin Law Review*, and other periodicals.